KU-017-847

SCOTTISH LIFE 1750–1945

Sydney Wood

Series editor Jon Nichol

Basil Blackwell

CONTENTS

INTRODUCTION

A shows part of Aberdeen in 1890. How can you tell that this is not a modern photograph? Old pictures contain clues to past life in Scotland. This book provides many different sorts of clue. Historians, like detectives, examine such clues (or *evidence*) to find out about the past. Look carefully at the evidence in the following pages in order to work out how Scottish people once lived and worked. Try and imagine what life must have been like for them. Compare their lives with yours today.

During the last 250 years life in Scotland has changed rapidly. **B** and **C** are two of the many clues that can be found in lists of figures.

When you have worked through the book you can explore the area where you live to see how it has changed since 1750. Visit your local museum to see the things people once used at home and work. Go to the local library to look for pictures, maps and books about your area. Talk to elderly people who can remember the area as it was 50 or more years ago. Walk round the streets looking at buildings, street names, bridges and any other clues that will help you see when and why the place where you live developed.

B **The number of people living in Scotland**

1755 – 1 250 000	**1911** – 4 760 000
1801 – 1 600 000	**1951** – 5 095 000
1831 – 2 400 000	**1971** – 5 227 000
1861 – 3 100 600	

C

1750: one in eight of Scotland's population was a town dweller

1850: one in three of Scotland's population was a town dweller

 ? ? ? ? ? ? ? ? ? ? ?

1 List all the clues in **A** that show it is an old picture.

2 Make up a list called 'Clues to Scotland's Past'. Put 'Old Pictures' as the first clue. Add as many as you can think of.

3 Write out **B** as a bar graph. How has the population changed in your area?

4 Look at **B** and **C**. Where did many of Scotland's increasing population go to live? Do you think this would cause any problems?

THE NEW FARMING

Scottish children born in the 1770s who lived to be over 70 saw great changes in the countryside. **A** is a map showing a small piece of Kincardine farmland. It was drawn in 1774. When map **B** was made, 50 years later, many changes had taken place there. Changes like this were taking place in all of Scotland's farming areas. Landowners wished to make money by finding better ways of growing more food to feed the country's growing population.

The church minister of Craill in Fife wrote:

C *Every improvement has been tried. In few places have the results of draining and trenching been more noticeable. 50 or 60 years ago a farmer had oxen to pull the plough. Now ploughs are at work drawn by a couple of horses; now the sound of the flail is seldom heard as every farmer has his threshing mill. Sea weed is used as manure. Lime and dung and bone dust are used.*

The crops follow the rotation – first potatoes or turnips, second wheat or barley, third beans or grass, fourth wheat or oats. Great attention is paid to the quality and keeping of horses.

The men who worked to improve the land found it was a very hard struggle. A farm worker called James Allan explains how he helped improve a piece of poor ground:

D *First we opened a trench, then we peeled the turf off the next strip and buried it in the trench. Then we slackened stones from the earth. The new field got a dressing of guano (fertilizer). The stones were used to make field drains and dykes . . .*

Many jobs on the farm were done by hand. Farmers with enough money had horse or water-powered threshing mills or hired a machine like **E**.

The farm workers' day was long and tiring:

F *The young ploughman had so little enjoyment in those days. Up at five in the morning and out to groom and feed their horses, then in again taking turns to make the porridge which was practically all they lived on. Then out to work with their horses from dawn to dusk with perhaps brose (boiling vegetable water poured on oatmeal) or another plate of porridge at dinner time and the same again in the evening.*

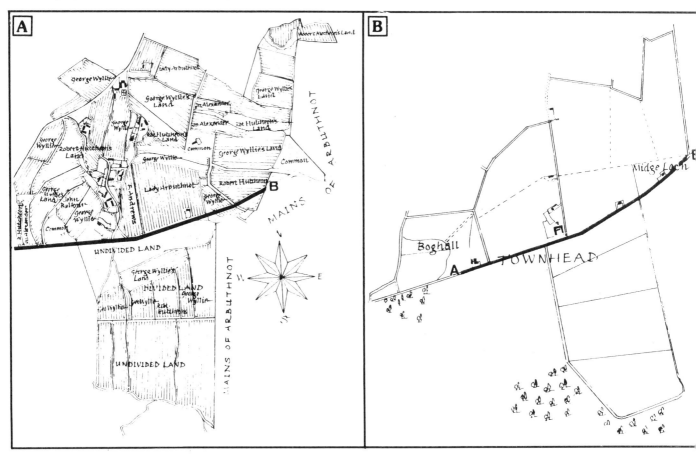

E

Farm workers with a steam threshing machine in the 1890s

Occasionally they would treat themselves to a loaf and butter or perhaps one of their mothers would give them a pot of home-made jam.

After work, the unmarried men went back to a room in the farm building called a *bothy*. **G** shows their clothing and the open fire used for cooking. The men are using wooden bowls and horn spoons to eat with. One of them sits on a wooden *kist*. Oatmeal and clothes were kept in kists like this one.

Farmers hired the workers they needed at the spring and autumn 'feeing' markets held in towns and bigger villages. A farm worker remembers how people were hired:

H *The feein' markets? The farmer 'ad say "Ye feein' laddie?" He'd need a cattleman or*

G

something. Ye had a straw an' sitted on a dyke an' the farmers had a walk up an' doon an' they come an' seen a likely lad for something he would come an' fee ye. Ye'd spit out yer straw. Ye got a shillin' — Ye wis'na feed until ye'd got a shillin'.

? ? ? ? ? ? ? ? ? ? ? ?

1 Improve a farm! Look at the evidence and then list
  a Three sorts of fertilizers to put on the land.
  b Four different sorts of crops to grow.
  c One other improvement.

2 Imagine you are a 14-year-old boy who has just started farm work. Use **F** and **G** to write a letter home. Mention hours of work, clothes, food and cooking.

3 **C** describes changes on the land. What do you think farming must have been like before these changes took place?

4 Look at **H**. What sort of person do you think a farmer wanted to hire? What sort of farm do you think a farm worker preferred? Make up an interview between farmer and worker, to be acted in front of your class.

NEW VILLAGES

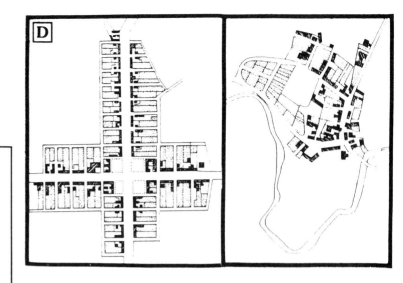

A

Village to be built at TONGUELAND

MR MURRAY of Broughton having determined to have a VILLAGE, has got a plan for the same by which there is to be a square in the middle and three streets and most excellent water would be brought into the square from a very fine spring.

In December 1793, readers of *The Dumfries Weekly Journal* might have seen advertisement **A**. Newspapers of the time often contained such advertisements, for many of Scotland's land-owners were busy creating villages.

Before 1750 there were few villages in Scotland. A landowner describes what these older villages were like:

B *The houses were not built according to any plan but scattered in every direction. The roads were bad, especially in wet weather as few were paved, and what added greatly to their miserable state was the abominable practice of placing the dunghill before their doors.*

The new farming meant that many poor cottagers lost their homes as the laird cleared the ground for his new fields. The new villages provided homes for these people. This is what happened to the Kincardine village of Laurencekirk.

C *When Lord Gardenstone made the purchase (in 1766) this village consisted of about 8 or 10 houses which were inhabited by some poor people. His Lordship let waste land for a village and in the course of 25 years he had the pleasure of seeing upwards of a hundred well-built houses and about 500 people set down upon this once barren moor, by which means he brought a market to the centre of his estate and encouraged manufacturers. About 30 weavers are now settled in this village, several carpenters, blacksmiths, thatchers, labourers etc. Lord Gardenstone has spent on making*

roads, building a handsome inn and a library which he furnished with well-chosen books.

New villages were usually quite a different shape from older places. The plans in **D** were drawn over 100 years ago. They show two Aberdeenshire villages, about a mile apart. Which is the newer, *planned* village? If you look carefully at villages today you can often work out whether or not they were planned. Look at the layout of the streets. Do they wander or are they very neatly organised?

The landowners hoped that many villagers would be craftsmen like those in **E** and **F**. These craftsmen would be able to do jobs for the farming folk who lived nearby. **G** lists the people who

F

worked in the Aberdeenshire village of Strichen in 1867.

Landowners also encouraged the holding of markets, like the one held in Huntly over 150 years ago:

H *There were women in grey cloaks with baskets on the arm containing butter, eggs, cheese and live fowls. Mingled with these are the wives, daughters and domestic servants of the town's people purchasing the week's food; in the middle of the square are cart loads of peat among which there may be a few loads of coal.*

Between 1750 and 1850 Scotland's villages grew in size and number. But there were too few of them to take in all of the country's increasing population. Many Scots had to leave the countryside and go to towns to seek work in factories.

G

3 church ministers	1 builder
2 church schools	1 saw miller
2 parish schools (boys and girls separate)	2 saddlers
	1 doctor
1 bank	1 brewer
2 blacksmiths	2 coopers
2 booksellers	1 druggist
6 boot and shoemakers	2 butchers
4 tailors	9 grocers and drapers
1 watchmaker	4 innkeepers
4 wrights (wheel makers)	1 corn miller

? ? ? ? ? ? ? ? ? ? ? ?

1 You have been looking, in this section, at different sorts of historical evidence. One sort of evidence is directories. List three more you have seen here.

2 Use the evidence to answer the following questions:

   a What did many people burn on fires instead of coal?

   b What were the roofs of some village and countryside houses made of?

   c What did blacksmiths fit round wooden cart wheels to stop them wearing away?

   d What were shops called that would be known today as chemists?

3 Why does Stuartfield, **D**, have a large space in the middle of it?

4 Imagine you are a laird trying to get people to come to the village of Kirkton. Make up a newspaper advertisement that will persuade people to move there.

5 Imagine you are the shoemaker in **E**. Write out a description of your thoughts as you work. Mention: the old days when the village was small and untidy (see **B**); the new laird, the new plans and houses and new people; the boot mending work you are doing and your friends in the village.

FACTORY LIFE

In the late eighteenth century, more and more people in Scotland earned their living from making things instead of by farming. A traveller wrote in 1774:

A *Within these few years Scotland has worn a very different appearance from what it formerly did. The manufactories now established in many parts of the country are all in a very flourishing condition. The linen trade has had great improvments made to it.*

For years many country people had earned extra money by making *yarn* (thread) and cloth from flax or wool. They worked at home using simple hand or foot powered machines like the one in **B**. But cloth making was changing in the late eighteenth century. New machines, worked by water or steam power, could spin much more rapidly than the old simple machines. The new machines were usually gathered together in factories, **C**. Many factories now produced cotton cloth.

Workers in the new factories sometimes had miserable lives:

D *When I went to a spinning mill I was about seven years of age. I had to get out of bed every morning at five o'clock, commence work at half past five, stop at nine for breakfast, begin again at half past nine, work until two (which was the dinner hour) start again at half past two and continue until half past seven at night. I was paid one shilling and sixpence per week.*

In one mill near Dundee the owner had bothies (huts) *where he lodged his workers. His mill was kept going 17 and 19 hours a day. To accomplish this, meal hours were almost done away with and women were employed to boil potatoes and carry them in baskets and the children had to swallow a potato hastily. At this mill boys and girls were often found sleeping on stairs.*

E *Robert Arnot was in 1826 overseer at Baxter's Mill, Dundee, where he saw the boys when too late of a morning, dragged naked from their beds by the overseers, and even by the master, with their clothes in their hands, to the mill where they put them on and the boys were strapped (beaten) naked as they got out of bed.*

A few owners provided healthy living and working conditions. The most famous of these was

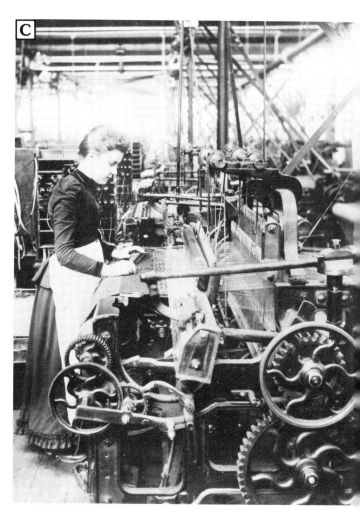

Robert Owen's New Lanark mills

Robert Owen who had mills at New Lanark, see **F**. In 1833 a doctor wrote a report on these mills:

G *New Lanark Mills are particularly clean and carefully kept, there are even blinds at the southern windows. A most extraordinary degree of attention is devoted to the education of the children of the workers. They are taught reading, writing, geography, music, dancing etc. in fine spacious rooms. I saw 8 young persons from 10 to 13 dance a quadrille.*

Most textile factories used large numbers of children. Owen explained to a questioner how they should be treated:

H *'At what age do you take children into your Mills?'*
'At 10 and upwards.'
'What are the regular hours of work?'
'10¾ hours.'
'Why do you not employ children at an earlier age?'
'Because I consider it would be harmful to the children and not beneficial to the owners.'

More and more of Scotland's growing population now lived in factory towns. British factories led the world in making goods cheaply.

Early factories used water power, but by 1800 many were changing to steam power. This meant that much more coal was needed from Scotland's mines.

?????????????

Imagine you have been left money by a rich uncle. You want to use it to set up a cloth-making business. First, you need to decide:

a Are you going to use hand workers, a water-powered mill or a steam-powered mill?
b Where will you build your mill – in a city, a town, the countryside? Should it be by a river?
c How many hours a day should the mill-hands work? (Remember: you will have to compete with other mills)
d How will you let people know it is time to start work?
e Will you help your workers, like Robert Owen (**G** and **H**), or treat them like the Dundee mill-owners (**D** and **E**)?

Give reasons for your answers.

DOWN THE MINE

A Tons of coal produced, 1750 – 1850

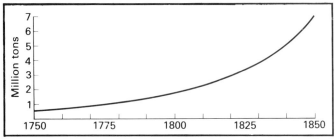

A shows that Scottish coal mines greatly increased production between 1750 and 1850. Much more coal was needed to heat the homes of a growing population, and to drive the steam engines found in factories and mines, on railways and in boats.

Coal miners had to work very hard. Until 1799 they were not free to work where they wanted. They belonged to the owner who first signed them up for his pit. The *hewers* (men who cut coal) worked like the miner in **B**. Their wives and children were *bearers*. They took away the coal – down the passages and up to the surface.

In 1842 a group of officials called Commissioners investigated Scotland's mines. Their report showed pictures of people at work, **C**. They spoke to the workpeople and wrote down what they said:

D *I work at Loanhead Colliery, have done so upwards of 2 years. Father has been dead 10 years. We go to work at four in the morning and return at two, sometimes five. When I work all night I gang at 5 or 6 in the evening and return 5 or 6 in the morning. I pick at the coal wall, it is gai sair work. We have no holidays but what we make ourselves. Bad air frequently stops one working below.*

David Burnside, 12 years old, coal hewer

E *Father gangs at 2 in the morning, I gang with the women at 5 and come up at 5 at night; work all the night on Fridays and come away at 12 in the day. I carry coal in a creel; the weight is usually a hundredweight. The roof is very low; I have to bend my back and legs and the water comes frequently up to the calves of my legs; often obliged to scramble out when bad air was in the pit.*

Janet Cumming, 11 years old, coal bearer

The Commissioners' report shocked the Members of Parliament. In 1842 they passed the *Mines Act*, which brought about changes in mine work. **F** is a poster which a colliery owner pinned up at his pit to tell the workpeople about the new law. A woman told officials, in 1844, how the Act had changed her life:

G *While working in the pit I was worth 7 shillings a week out of which we had to pay 2 shillings and 6 pence to a woman looking after the younger bairns. I used to take them to her house at 4 o'clock in the morning. Then there was a shilling a week for washing. The other children broke things, they did not go to school when they were sent. When I came home in the evening everything was to do after the day's labour and I was so tired I had no heart for it; no fire lit, nothing cooked, no water fetched, the house dirty.*

F

NOTICE.

In consequence of the Act of the 5th and 6th Queen Victoria, cap. 99, His Grace the Duke of Hamilton hereby intimates, that from and after the 10th current, no *Females*, under 18 years of age, nor after the 1st of March next, shall any *Females*, of whatever age, be employed in the underground operations at Redding Colliery. He farther intimates, that from and after the 1st day of March next, no *Male* persons, under the age of 10 years, shall be employed under-ground at said Colliery ; and he strictly prohibits all his Colliers and Workmen, at said Colliery, from, in any way, taking the assistance of any such in the underground operations which are being performed by them.

(Signed) **JOHN JOHNSTON,**
MANAGER.

REDDING COLLIERY,
1st November, 1842.

A. Johnston, Printer, Falkirk.

Scotland's miners produced coal mainly for Scottish homes and factories. Coal is heavy and hard to move. The success of the industry depended on improvements being made to travel.

1 Imagine you own a coal mine. You want to make your mine deeper and bigger so that more coal can be produced. Draw a plan to show how your shallow coal mine must be enlarged. Show how you will support the roofs of the passages and how you will get fresh air into the pits. How will you stop the mine from flooding? How will miners travel up and down the pit?

2 Complete the sentences
   a The men who cut coal were called _____.
   b The people who carried coal were called _____.
   c Coal was carried in baskets called _____.
   d The Mines Act was in the year _____.

   e After the Act women, girls and boys under _____ years could not work-underground.

3 How much did the woman in **G** lose from her weekly wage?

4 Imagine you are one of the Commissioners. You have just visited Loanhead Colliery. Look at the pictures in **C**. Use them to describe in your own words what you see in the pit. Mention the work, the clothing, the dangers of life in the pit.

5 What do you think coal mine owners thought of evidence like **D**, **E** and **G**? What do you think they might have said in favour of using women and children in pits and in favour of the hours of work?

IRON-MAKERS

It is the year 1759. You are going into business as a maker of iron goods. Where should you build your business? What will you need in order to set up a works? You will have to think about the following facts:

1 In 1709, in England, Abraham Darby discovered how to use coke (from coal) to smelt iron, instead of charcoal (from timber).
2 Scottish coal and iron ore fields are in central Scotland.
3 Coal, iron ore and iron goods are heavy.
4 The roads of 1759 are uneven and rough. It is difficult to take heavy goods over them.
5 Iron goods are needed by people for tools, cooking pots etc.
6 Iron weapons are needed by the government, and by the governments of other countries.

Look at the map of Scotland on page 64 of this book. Make a rough sketch of the map. Mark on it where you will set up in business. Below the map write your reasons for choosing this place. (Remember: you must think of who will buy your goods, how you can move heavy goods and how you can smelt iron ore.)

In 1759 three men were thinking about exactly this problem. Their names were Samuel Garbett, John Roebuck and William Cadell. Look at the canal map on page 16 and find a place called Carron. This is where these men set up what soon became Scotland's greatest ironworks. How does their choice compare with yours?

In 1769 a visitor described the Carron Ironworks:

A (They) *lie about a mile from Falkirk and are the greatest of their kind in Europe – they were founded about 8 years ago, before which time there was not a single house there, the country was a moor. At present the buildings are of vast extent and about 1200 men are employed. The iron is smelted from the stone, then cast into cannon, pots and all sorts of things . . . Carron Wharf* (for loading ships) *lies on the Forth and is useful to the works. The canal likewise begins in this neighbourhood.*

We can find out more about what the works made from a list written in 1761, **B**. Carron became especially famous for the guns that it made. In 1784 a French visitor to the works saw guns being made there for sale all over the world:

C *The place was covered with cannons, mortars, bombs, balls and carronades (a kind of gun). Amidst these machines of war gigantic cranes, levers and pulleys serving to move so many heavy loads are erected. Their movements, the creaking of pulleys, the continual noise of hammers, everything presents a sight as new as it is interesting. Under the sheds we saw cannons, guns, etc, destined for Russia and the Emperor.*

Four furnaces, each 45 feet in height, for melting the ore, devoured both day and night enormous masses of coal and metal. Each disgorges (pours out) every 6 hours streams of

B GOODS manufactured and fold by the **CARRON-Company.**

CYLINDERS for Fire Engines, from 24 to 80 Inches diameter, (bored,) with Bottoms and finking Pipes - -
Piftons, turned, Steam Veffels and Steam Pipes - -
Bored Pipes from 4 to 30 Inches diameter - -
Caft Iron Chains, from 10 to 200 Weight a Link - -
Wrought Iron Pins for ditto properly fitted, 3½ d. per lib. -
Bars and Bearers for Fire Engines, of caft Iron - -
Doors and Frames for ditto of caft Iron - -
Cranks of all fizes for Water Engines of ditto - -
Cannon from 2 Pounders to 42 Pounders - - -
Swivels, Mortars, and Cohorns of all Sizes - - -
Cannon-ball from ¼ Pounders to 42 Pounders - - -
Boilers from 15 to 500 Gallons Weight lib. per Gallon
Doors and Frames for Furnaces of all fizes - - -
Garden Rollers from 5 hundred to 40 hundred Weight -
Rails for ftairs and Balluftrades of any Pattern - - -
Stove Grates of caft Iron, polifhed and fitted with Backs, &c. from 12 to 20 Inches wide - - - -
Stove-grate Fronts from 15 lib. to 30 lib. Weight, 12 to 20 Inches wide
Kitchen Grates with fquare and pyramidical Pillars,
Purgatories or Afh-Grates, Weight from lib. to lib. polifhed
Stewing Stoves from 6 to 12 Inches diameter, round, octagon or fquare
Perpetual Ovens from 16 to 20 Inches diameter, round or octagon, with Dampers, &c.
Cranes for Kitchens from lib. to lib. polifhed, unpolifhed
Sad Irons or fmoothing Irons, from 4½ lib. to 10½ lib. per Pair, polifhed
Box Irons No. 1. No. 2. No. 3. No. 4. No. 5.
Heaters for ditto - - - - -

liquid iron. Each furnace is supplied by air pumps, the air uniting into one pipe and directed towards the flame.

Between 1759 and 1815 the British were involved in several wars. These wars helped the Carron Ironworks to prosper. **D** is a photograph of the Carron yard taken in 1870. The metal pans and grates stacked there are evidence that Carron did not just make guns.

By 1820 seven more ironworks like Carron had been set up in Scotland. They made machines for factories as well as all sorts of smaller objects. Scotland became a world-famous centre for goods made from iron, especially ships and railway engines.

The Carron works grew up near the sea because it was difficult to move bulky iron and coal except by boat. But alongside the growth of factories, mines and ironworks a great change in transport was also taking place in Scotland between 1750 and 1860.

? ? ? ? ? ? ? ? ? ? ? ?

1 List at least five different things made at Carron.

2 Why were the Carron Works set up on that particular site?

3 Look at **C**. What do you think the air pumps were for?

4 Using all the information in this section, design an advertisement for Carron Ironworks dated 1800, telling people what the works can make.

5 Look in your area for things made of iron. They often have stamped on them the name of the ironworks. Look for metal bridges, for covers and grids in pavements and gutters, for railings, gates and pipes.

TURNPIKES

In 1750 travel in Scotland was difficult. James Anderson of Aberdeenshire, writing in 1794, explained:

A *About 40 or 50 years ago there was no road in this country on which wheels of any kind could be dragged, weighty burdens were carried on horseback. (Today) the roads continue to be in such a miserable state that but for a few months in summer, it is impossible to drive a carriage with more than half a load. Till good roads be established agriculture and other improvements can never proceed with energy.*

Factory owners, coal mine owners, shop-keepers and traders all suffered, too, from the difficulties travellers faced in the eighteenth century. But who would pay for better roads?

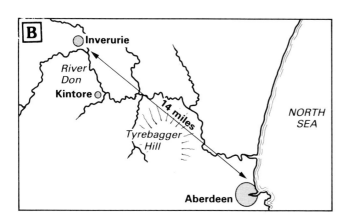

Imagine you live in the small town of Inverurie **B**. You want to do business with the port of Aberdeen but there is no good road and the government won't pay for one. How would you find the money to pay for the road? How would you get your money back? What problems would lie in the way of road building? How would you overcome them? All over Scotland problems like these faced people who wanted to buy and sell goods. Their answer was to join together to raise enough money to pay for the building of new roads. These roads were called *turnpikes*. The idea for them was copied from England.

A local minister, George Skene Keith, watched the Inverurie turnpike being built:

C *An open space 14 feet wide and 14 inches deep was left in the middle of the road. This was filled up with granite which was broken into small pieces and is called 'metalling'. A quantity of gravel or sandy soil was laid on top about an inch deep and is called 'blinding'. The rain gradually washes a considerable part of this down among the stones. It is not till carts or carriages have pounded the stones that the road becomes agreeable to a traveller.*

The men who had paid for the road charged tolls to pay the cost of building and running it. Every

E   **Toll charges on the Inverurie turnpike**

6 horses drawing any	coach,	omnibus etc with 4 wheels	6/-
5 " " " " " " " " "	4/-
2 " " " " " " " " "	1/-
2 " " " chaise,	gig,	etc with 2 wheels	1/-
1 " " " " " " " " "	8d
6 " " " waggon,	cart	etc with 6 wheels	8/-
4 " " " " " " " " "	5/-
2 " " " " " " " " "	2/-
2 horses drawing an empty farmers cart	6d
Every horse, with or without rider	3d
Cattle, oxen, horses (unshod), per score	10d
Calves, hogs, sheep, lambs, goats, per score	5d

six miles small *toll houses* like **D** were built by the roadside. A toll-house-keeper lived here and collected money from travellers. **E** shows the toll charges for the Inverurie turnpike. A gate blocked the road to stop travellers galloping past without paying. Up and down the new turnpike trundled farmers' carts, quarry wagons and all sorts of other vehicles. Stage coach services like **F** carried passengers and mail and stopped at the many inns built alongside the turnpikes. The Reverend Davidson remembered Inverurie's coaches:

G *They were bright objects, their scarlet-coated bugler-guard and lively four horse teams were seen or heard almost daily . . . Inverurie had a coach of its own − 'The Banks of Ury'. It was the property of its coachman, Geordie Gray. His temper was uncertain and unsettled by drams and when irritable he thought nothing of refusing passage to a customer. He silenced passengers by turning his back to his horses and driving for a while without seeing either them or the road. When the railway was opened the coach disappeared.*

Turnpike roads spread across Scotland, linking together all the main towns and cities. People who could afford the cost could now travel speedily and fairly comfortably. But traders wanting to shift heavy goods found turnpikes dear to use. They needed another kind of improved travel to help their businesses.

? ? ? ? ? ? ? ? ? ? ? ?

1 Fill in the blanks in the sentences.
  a A road that travellers paid to use was called a _____ .
  b The man who collected the money lived in a _____ .
  c The stones used to make the road were called _____ .
  d These roads were ruined by the coming of the _____ .

2 Imagine you are a surveyor who is planning the Inverurie turnpike. Look at **B** and **C**. Draw a plan of the road from Aberdeen to Inverurie and label it to show where there will have to be expensive work (like bridge-building).

3 Look around your area for toll houses. Measure one and draw a plan of it. Why do you think its front windows are so oddly arranged?

4 Look at **A**. Why were people prepared to pay for roads with their own money?

5 Look at **F**. Imagine you are a reporter for the 'Aberdeen Journal' who has been on Geordie Gray's coach. Describe your journey. Mention what the coach looked like, where the passengers sat and how the coachman behaved.

CANALS

For many businessmen the answer to the problem of moving heavy goods came when waterways (canals) were dug, along which barges could travel. Scottish canal-building began in about 1770 and copied work going on in England. By this time the increasing demand for coal, stone, slate, grain and other products made canal-building worthwhile. Most canals were in the Glasgow and Edinburgh area. Here they were near the coalfields and big cities. Look at the map on page 64 to see where there were other canals. Why would it have been difficult to build canals in many parts of Scotland?

Why build canals?

A *The grand benefits to the community by the opening of the Union Canal are . . . First heavy goods are now brought to Edinburgh from Glasgow and the West of England at a very trifling expense. Second, new fields of coal are open to Edinburgh consumers and coal is about half the price formerly charged. Third the boats bringing coal, stones etc are loaded with the dung of Edinburgh by which means the grounds*

in Linlithgow and Stirlingshire are easily fertilised by the cheap manure.

A was written about the Union Canal in 1832. Now look at **B** and **C**. List as many reasons as possible why canal-building took place.

The men who built the canals were called *navigators* or 'navvies'. Many of them were Irishmen. They often lived in miserable huts:

D *There are huts erected by Irish labourers. One of them, with the exception of a few sticks, is composed entirely of rotten straw; its size would not suffice for a pig sty and its form is that of a beehive only it is more conical. The smoke which does not escape at the door goes through every part of the structure which thus presents the picture of a hayrick on fire.*

E is a list of workers on the Forth-Clyde canal. All sorts of skilled workmen were needed. In places the canals had to be built over sloping ground, and locks were needed to raise the canal level. A traveller watched work on a lock, in 1819:

F *Went to look at the locks. It was a most impressive sight. Men, horses and machines at work digging, walling and puddling (lining canal with clay to keep in the water) going on, men wheeling barrows, horses drawing stones.*

B

1770	Cost to a customer of buying a hundredweight of coal in Glasgow — 3d.
	Cost to a customer of buying a hundredweight of coal in Monkland — 1d.
	Cost of moving a hundredweight of coal from Monkland to Glasgow — 1d.

E

14	contractors (in charge of groups of workers)
25	carpenters
81	quarrymen
130	masons
419	labourers

C   **The first Scottish canals**

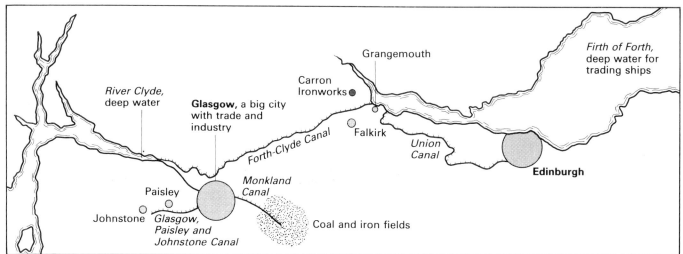

G

The iron for a pair of lock-gates was lying on the ground.

Sometimes canals had to be carried on aqueducts over rivers or roads. **G** shows an aqueduct on the Union Canal.

Many people of the time were amazed when they saw a canal. This account of an aqueduct was sent to the *Scots Magazine* in 1805:

H *The canal was to be an object of great curiosity, having never seen anything like it. Here it is carried above the road and the traveller has the sensation of water rolling and vessels sailing over his head. The breadth of the water, the opening and shutting of the gates of the locks, with the vessels which glided smoothly and silently along, presented an interesting spectacle.*

The canal-building age lasted about 50 years. By the 1840s canals were threatened by a competitor – railways. Travel by canal was slow. Canals were difficult to build in hilly areas. Railways offered travel that was speedier than turnpikes and they could also transport the bulky goods carried in canal barges.

? ? ? ? ? ? ? ? ? ? ?

1   Use **C** and the map on page 64 to list all the canals in Scotland.

2   From what you have read in the last chapter who might have been against canals?

3   Write out a list of the different sorts of evidence you have used to find out about canals.

4   Look at **E**. Make up a poster as if you were a canal engineer advertising for workers. Explain what you want the different workers to do.

5   Using **D**, draw a picture of a navvy's hut.

6   You can see from **F** and **H** how canals and canal-building impressed people. Write a newspaper article called 'The Canal Opens'. Describe the struggle to build the canal, the difficulties the navvies faced and the opening voyage by a barge full of important people.

RAILWAYS

The building of Scotland's modern railway system started in the 1830s. The success of English railways encouraged Scottish businessmen. These accounts come from two newspapers of 1841:

A *The rock is swarming with workmen and the continual clank of the thousand hammers is only interrupted by the roar of hundreds of blasts, fired in succession, hurling terrific masses of rock high into the air.*

B *Everywhere along the works the pick, the spade, and the hammer are busily used by bands of sturdy Irishmen. The constant moving to and fro of the wagons adds much to the bustle of the scene.*

D **The Scottish railway network in 1900**

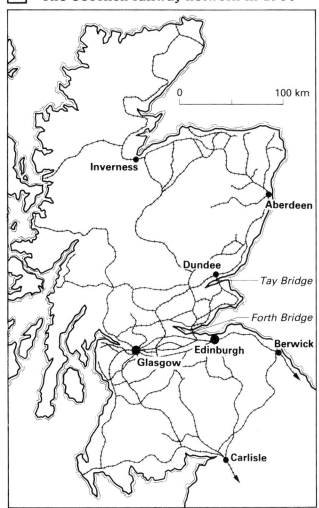

When the navvies finished a line they sometimes enjoyed a free feast:

C *It appears that the workmen employed on the railway, 300 to 400 of them, received about 90 gallons of whisky with bread, cheese, hams etc as a treat in honour of the opening. Some seized whole loaves and hams while others could not taste a scrap. This gave rise to complaints and a general battle followed.*

By 1900 many railway companies had been formed and a network of track covered the country, **D**.

The opening of a new line was an exciting event. **E** shows the opening in 1831 of a line from Glasgow to Garnick. Both a passenger and a goods train are on the tracks. Notice the engine.

Many writers of the time tried to express their feelings when they saw a new railway open. One of them was William MacGonagall. He lived in Dundee and spent much of his time writing dreadful poems. Here he explains the importance of a new line between Dundee and nearby Newport:

F *Success to the Newport Railway*
Along the braes of the Silvery Tay
And to Dundee straightway
Across the Railway Bridge o' the Silvery Tay
Which was opened on the 12th of May
In the year of our Lord 1879
Which will clear all expenses in a very short time
Because the thrifty housewives of Newport
To Dundee will often resort
Which will be to them profit and sport
By bringing cheap tea, bread and jam
And also some of Lipton's ham.

In 1845 the *Scottish Railway Gazette* reported:

G *All parts of the country will become more opened up. The land of the interior will, by a system of cheap and rapid transport for manure and produce, become almost as valuable as that upon the coast. The man of business can as easily join his family at a distance of 10 or 12 miles as could formerly be done at 2 or 3 miles. Fish was not available a few miles from the coast: wherever the railway goes it will now be carried.*

How do you think the turnpike and canal companies felt about this?

The railways ruined several canal companies

E

and ended the long-distance stage coach services. But they brought new trade for local coaches and carts. Most importantly, they opened up Scotland, linked its different areas together and connected places in Scotland with places in England. They made it far easier for people to travel, on business or holiday. They made it possible for goods bought in one part of Scotland to be sent for sale many miles away.

Early railway travellers needed to be tough. What clues to the problems of railway travel can you see in **E**? There were quite a number of railway accidents. The most famous happened in 1879. The two-year-old bridge over the River

Tay at Dundee collapsed in a storm. A train was travelling over the bridge at the time, and it tumbled into the river. 75 people died. **H** shows the scene after the disaster, with divers going down to search the wreckage.

H

? ? ? ? ? ? ? ? ? ? ?

1 Complete this poster, using **A** and **B**.
BECOME A NAVVY
We need men who are _____. Men able to use tools like _____ and _____. Men who know how to blow up rocks with _____. Good wages. When the line is finished there will be a feast with free _____ and _____!

2 Look at **D**. Why are most of the railway lines in central Scotland? Look at a modern map with railways on it. Are there fewer or more lines today?

3 How did railways alter people's lives? Look at **F** and **G**. Write a list of goods that the writers thought would be cheaper and easier to get because of railways. What other things might the writers have added to the list?

4 Choose either **E** or **H** and imagine you are present at one of these events. Write a letter to a friend describing the sights and sounds of the scene and the conversations you have with other people there.

WHY DID GLASGOW GROW?

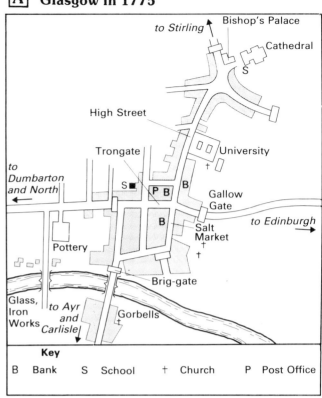

A **Glasgow in 1775**

to Stirling
Bishop's Palace
Cathedral
S
High Street
University
Trongate
to Dumbarton and North
S
P B
B
Gallow Gate
to Edinburgh
Pottery
Salt Market
Brig-gate
Glass, Iron Works
to Ayr and Carlisle
Gorbells

Key

B Bank   S School   † Church   P Post Office

During the nineteenth century Glasgow became Scotland's biggest city. When did it grow? Why did it grow? Find out by looking at the different clues in this section, and in earlier parts of this book.

1 Look carefully at the evidence on these pages. What different sorts of evidence can you see here?

2 Look at the date when each clue was written or drawn. Write a list of all the clues with their dates, in the correct order. Your work should begin

    a Picture, 1764
    b Thomas Pennant's visit, 1769
    c Map, 1775

Continue the list.

3 Look at the earlier maps in the book. What reasons do they suggest as to why Glasgow was a well placed city?

4 Look at **A**, **D** and **F**. How can you tell from these that Glasgow was an important place even before it began to grow rapidly? Why would lots of people come to the city?

5 From **B** and **F** find out a reason why Glasgow grew between 1750 and 1775. Why did this stop being important in later years?

6 Compare **D** and **E**. How has Glasgow changed in this time?

7 Read **G**, **H**, **J** and **K**. What brought people to Glasgow to find work?

8 Now put all these different pieces of evidence together. Imagine you are an elderly person who lives in Glasgow in 1850. You are telling your grandson about all the changes you have seen in your city over your long life. Say whether you think the changes have made Glasgow a better place to live in.

B **Tobacco brought into Glasgow from America**

1755 15 200 000 pounds (weight)
1775 45 863 000 pounds
(1775–1783 war between Britain and North America)
1795 2 731 000 pounds

C **Population of Glasgow, 1750–1871**

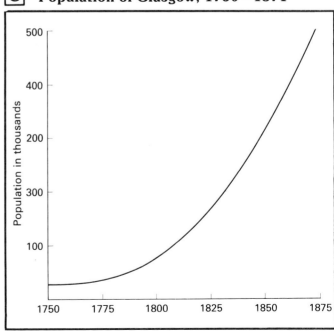

Population in thousands

500
400
300
200
100

1750   1775   1800   1825   1850   1875

Glasgow in 1764

Glasgow in the 1820s

F Thomas Pennant's Glasgow visit, 1769.
Glasgow. The best built of any second-rate city I saw: the houses of stone and in good taste. The market places are great ornaments in this city, the fronts being done in a very fine taste. Some are for meal, greens, fish and flesh. The old bridge over the Clyde consists of eight arches. The great imports of the city are tobacco and sugar.

G J. Denholm's History of Glasgow, written in 1804.
The main exports to America are manufactures, coal, fish. To Europe sugar, coffee, cotton and rum. Glasgow imports from the West Indies and America coffee, cotton, sugar, rum; from Spain and Portugal wines; from the Baltic wood, iron, flax, hemp, tar and wheat.

H In 1820 James Cleland wrote:

During 1818 there were 105 million yards of cloth manufactured in Glasgow and neighbourhood and half of these goods were exported. There are 16 works for weaving by power.

J In 1818 Robert Chapman wrote:
In the city there are 9 iron foundries and several works for making steam engines. Employed in different manufactures in Glasgow there are 73 steam engines. For this most useful engine our country is indebted to Mr (James) Watt, a native of Glasgow.

K In 1856 John Strang wrote:
Glasgow has the docks and port of Liverpool, the tall chimneys and manufactories of Manchester, the iron and engineering works of Birmingham, the pottery of Staffordshire, the shipbuilding of London, the coal trade of Tyne and Wear and handicrafts.

EDINBURGH, OLD AND NEW

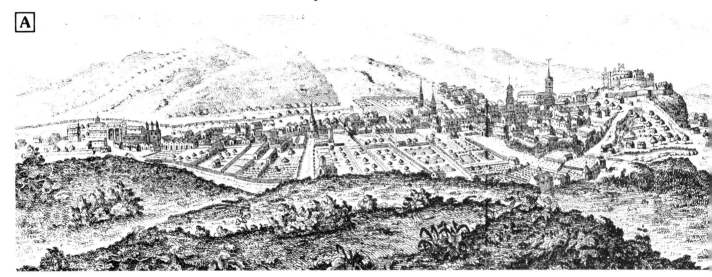

Edinburgh is Scotland's capital city. **A** is an early eighteenth century map of Edinburgh. Most old Scottish *burghs* (towns) were this sort of shape. Houses stretched along a High Street and up narrow *wynds* (lanes) leading off it **B**.

By 1752 Edinburgh was becoming very crowded. Some important people grumbled about it:

C *Placed on a ridge of a hill it has but one good street. The narrow lanes leading to the north and south, by reason of their steepness, narrowness and dirtiness, can only be considered as nuisances. The houses stand more crowded than in any other town in Europe and are built to a height that is almost incredible. Hence a great want of air, light and cleanliness. Hence many families, sometimes ten or a dozen, live overhead of each other in the same building (with) a common stair, constantly dark and dirty. The main street is blocked off with markets. Edinburgh ought to have set the first example of industry and improvement.*

They thought that Edinburgh needed to grow into new areas if it was to become a pleasanter place to live in. There was a competition to see who should plan the new town, and it was won by James Craig in 1767. The first thing that had to be built was a bridge to join the houses of the old town to open fields further north.

James Craig planned wide streets and squares, **D**. Architects then designed fine new buildings like **E**. In 1774 an English visitor saw this work taking place:

F *From the right of the High Street you pass over a very long bridge to the New Town. The New Town has been built upon one uniform plan. Great parts of this plan as yet remain to be executed. The houses are what they call here 'houses to themselves'. Such is the force of prejudice that there are many people who prefer*

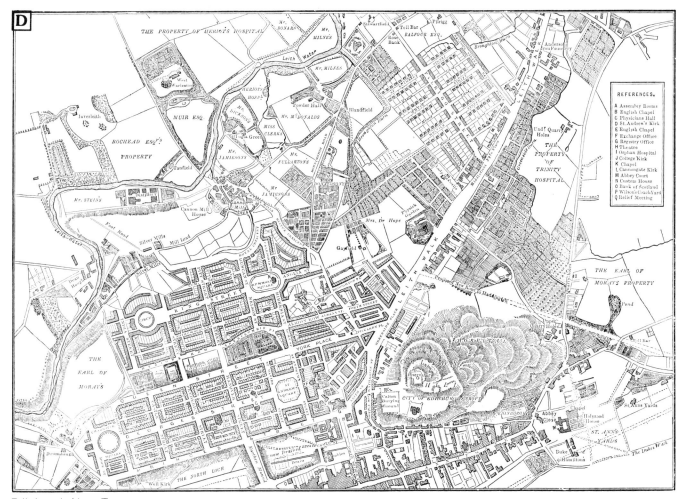

Edinburgh New Town

a little dark tenement on a sixth storey to the convenience of a whole house. In no town that I ever saw can such contrast be found betwixt the modern and ancient architecture.

Edinburgh soon became one of Europe's finest cities. If you are able to visit Edinburgh, notice how different the old and new towns still look.

?????????????

1 Compare **A** and **E**. What do they tell you about the old and new parts of the city? Which part do you think the poorer people would live in? Why?

2 Look at the houses in **B** and **E**. Make a list of all the differences between them that you can see.

3 Using the evidence on this page, design a poster asking people to come to a meeting about improving Edinburgh. On one half of the poster list 'What's wrong with our city'. On the other half list 'What we need'.

23

EXPLORING A CITY

During the nineteenth century several educated people left their comfortable large city homes to visit the crowded, poorer parts of Scotland's growing towns and cities. They wanted to find out how people lived who were much poorer than themselves.

Imagine you are going on such a journey of exploration. It is the year 1858. You are going into the poorest parts of Glasgow. Your guide is a man who calls himself 'Shadow'. It is late evening. The people stare at you as you walk into their *closes* (yards) **A**. What do you imagine they are thinking? You meet a little barefoot boy:

B *He implores us to buy a bawbee worth of matches.*

'Well my boy, what keeps you out so late as this?' 'To sell my matches'
'What is your name?' 'Johnny'
'How old are you?' 'Don't know. Guess I'm 7 or 8.'
'Is your father alive?' 'No'
'Is your mother alive?' 'Yes, but she's owre auld to dae onything. I've twa brithers and sisters.'
'What does your eldest brother do?' 'He gets auld papers and sells them.'
'What does your sister do?' 'She sells sticks.'
'Then how is your mother supported?' 'By us.'
'How many rooms have you?' 'One'
'How did you all sleep in one room when your father was ill?' 'Some of us stood up. We took turn aboot on the bed.'

You walk slowly on.

C *Following a plain but respectable-looking man up a filthy close we express our interest to him in exploring the locality.*
'Come on sir', he says, 'I'll let you see whaur we live.'

An aged woman opens the door bearing a candle in her hand. As we enter full of apologies, a group of half-dressed people collect around the fire-place.

'How do you manage' we say, 'to live in such a place, there must be at least 6 or 8 of you?'
'Deed sir' says the elderly dame, 'we're nae waur than our neighbours an' we dinna think onything aboot it.'

We glance again at the wretched hovel. A dirty candle stuck into the neck of a bottle shines light throughout the room. In a corner is a window, near the roof, just big enough to light a prison cell. On the floor are placed two beds. There is a large filthy pail, the urinal common to the entire household.

You come out and walk through other closes like **D** before leaving the area. Next day you go to the offices of *The Glasgow Herald* newspaper. There you look for articles about the city. You are especially interested in one written by a medical inspector in 1848:

E *The wynds and closes of Glasgow consist of narrow closes only 4 to 5 feet in width and of great length. The houses are so lofty the direct light of the sky never reaches a large part of the dwellings. There are large dunghills near the windows and doors, they hold the filth and offal of large masses of people until farmers can be bargained with for their removal. The sewers, where they exist, are pools polluting the air. I saw a backyard covered with several inches of green putrid water . . . There are no domestic conveniences (toilets) even in the loftiest tenements except a kind of wooden sink outside some stair window and communicating by a square wooden pipe with the surface of the court beneath. Down it is poured the entire filth of the household.*

F

? ? ? ? ? ? ? ? ? ? ?

1 A visit like this would have shocked a wealthy person. Write a letter to a newspaper. In it describe all the sights, sounds and smells of your visit.
  a Look at **A**, **D** and **F** to see how people dressed, how the closes were lit, where washing was hung out and where the people in the houses obtained their water.
  b Use **B** and **C** to describe how poor people are, what it is like in their rooms, what sort of furniture they have and how they light their rooms.
  c Use **E** to explain what the courtyards look like and smell like.
  d Put forward a plan to improve the poor people's living conditions.

2 Why do you think people had to live in such misery?

3 What sort of harmful results would follow from the presence of areas like this in cities?

4 Who might be able to improve areas like this?

AT SCHOOL

C The Education Act, 1872

1 All children shall go to school from 5–13
2 School boards to be elected all over Scotland to be in charge of schools
3 All pupils to be examined every year by Inspectors
4 Head teachers to be properly able to teach

In 1867 the government sent a group of important men to look at Scotland's schools. They were called the Argyll Commission. In the cities they found several schools like **A**. Parents who had to go to work paid to send their children to such schools.

A *The school is kept in a dank cellar in which, when we visited, 35 children were assembled. The smell was hot, foul and oppressive. A drunken fellow, a friend of the master, was lying asleep across one of the benches at which the children were sitting. We selected 3 pupils, picked out as the farthest advanced, we found it was with difficulty they could spell the words, the pronouncing of which was hopeless.*

There were also many excellent schools in Scotland. Every parish had to have a school, and these were usually well-run. **B** gives information about one of these schools. But there were too few parish schools for the country's growing population. Also, many parents kept their children away from school for part of the year and sent them out to earn money. The government decided to bring in a new law to improve education **C**.

Schools like **A** soon disappeared. Most children went to classrooms that looked like **D**. The number of children in a class was large, often

B The parish school of Fraserburgh in 1871

Number of classrooms – 3	
Number of teachers – 3	
Number of pupils – 266	
Subjects taught	– Elementary (for all pupils): Reading, Writing, Arithmetic
	– Higher: Higher English, Maths, Grammar, French, German, Latin, Science, Sewing, Music

School fees – Standard		
	I	2/6d a quarter
	II	3/- a quarter
	III	3/6d a quarter
	IV	4/- a quarter
	V	4/6d a quarter
	VI	5/- a quarter

Extra for Latin, Greek and Maths: 1/6d a subject or 2/6d for all three.

around 60. Amy Stewart Fraser looks back and remembers her days in Glen Gairn School in Aberdeenshire, during the 1890s:

E *Our school was a bare barn of a place. It was cold. In winter we (took turns) to group ourselves round the fire . . . Girls entered by one porch, boys by a similar one. Scholars sat on narrow benches facing scarred tops hardly worthy of the name of desk. All grades were taught by a single teacher. Each group stood in turn round the teacher's chair and answered questions. My first teacher used the tawse freely and unkindly, reducing even the biggest boys to tears as she lashed round their bare feet.*

The 3 Rs, Reading, 'Riting, 'Rithmetic, were hammered home by repetition. We received instruction in geography and history; these consisted of feats of memory, names, long lists, strings of dates. Our classwork was done on slates. After learning to write on slates we were promoted to copy books, pen and ink, dipping the pen in the inkwell sunk in the desk, we copied sayings like 'Honesty is the best policy'. No crayons, coloured pencils or paints were used.

Normally only the children who lived near the school went home at midday, the rest brought their 'pieces', bread soaked with jam. Scholars took it in turns to fetch water from a well.

Every week, headteachers had to note down any important events that had happened in their school. This is part of the logbook for a school in the Kincardine village of Banchory:

F 1873, 19th Dec. *Younger classes at present taught by monitors (older pupils). Require more attention.*
1876, Dec. 12th. *Sent 2 boys to the village and got a good heavy 'tag' or 'tawse'.*
1878, Oct. 18th. *The Latin and Greek classes are progressing well. Geography well learned. Children learn French eagerly and with ability – save for the pronunciation which is bad owing to the local accent.*
1878, March 21st. *Owing to rumours of*

D

diphtheria being in school most children have been kept at home.

1883, Oct. 15th. *First fires of season lighted, supply of coals having arrived.*

1885, Aug. 14th. *Weather so bad it was impossible to hold picnic outside and the Misses Davidson came to school and served them with tea and cake. The scholars were in great glee.*

1888, July 20th. *Strawberries are beginning to ripen and boys and girls are employed to gather them. Turnip hoeing also takes away some.*

1895, March 25th. *A piano is in use and gymnastics have been attempted with the arms alone, the apparatus would be improved by the addition of dumb bells.*

1897, Feb. 1st. *William Craven sat on the playground wall, daring the Janitor's best efforts to catch him.*

1897, Feb. 11th. *The boy William Craven was expelled.*

Logbooks like **F** are still kept today. Perhaps your school has old logbooks that you can study.

??????????????

1 Use the evidence to work out:
a two reasons for the 1872 Education Act
b the average size of a class in 1871 in Fraserburgh Parish School
c the cost for a year of a pupil in Standard V who did Latin, Greek and Mathematics.

2 Look at **D**. List all the differences you can find between the appearance of the people and classroom shown here and your classroom today.

3 Imagine you are teacher at Glen Gairn. Look at **F** to see how logbooks are written. Then write several entries for the Glen Gairn logbook. Use the information in **E** to help you. For example:
'1894, June 7th. *Used the tawse to beat several boys who had been ill-mannered*'

POOR PEOPLE

Today, when people are too young, old, or ill to work, or can't find a job, how do they manage to get money so that they do not starve?

In early nineteenth century Scotland the poor got very little help. Some people were concerned about this, and reports were sent to the government:

A Reports on the poor from different places in Scotland, 1844

Huntly doctor *It is not so much lack of medical care that hits the poor as want of clothing, insufficient food and bad houses.*

Huntly church minister *Friday is the licensed day for begging in Huntly. Those who beg used to have badges but the people consider badges a mark of shame.*

Peterhead doctor *Illnesses develop from no other cause than the filth and wretchedness of the people and particularly lack of enough nourishing food.*

Kingussie minister *The poor go from house to house begging and getting meal. Those not able to get about are very badly off. The Kirk (church) elders look after them. The poor live on meal and potatoes. In one year near 100 left for Australia.*

Duthill local farmer *They have no money for the poor except church collections. The poor beg, there is no provision for them in sickness. Their houses are miserable hovels, their bedding is a wisp of straw.*

Rothiemurchus minister *Some poor go begging, they travel as far as 20 miles. There is a great inclination to emigrate to Canada.*

B Poor Law reform 1845

1 Scotland was made up of many small areas called parishes. Each parish had to choose a 'Parochial Board' to care for the poor.
2 The Boards could gather money from local people able to afford to pay a poor rate.
3 Inspectors worked for the Boards, checking all the poor who asked for help to see if they really were in desperate need.

C The Fraserburgh Parochial Board Minutes

1846 *Agreed to buy 2 blankets for the use of the poor. A.S.'s application for help refused. He has 5 shillings a week pension and a wife and 2 children able to work.*
Agreed to open a soup kitchen. The Board will consider all applications for soup from those unable to support themselves and their families because of the high price of food.

1847 *The following applications were agreed. Widow of W.C. to receive 2 shillings and a stone of meal weekly.*

1851 *Help with school fees to Widow B.'s 2 children.*

1858 *A claim for a pair of shoes from Widow C. The Inspector was directed to afford (give) a pair to her.*
Widow B.'s application – the Inspector was directed to afford her tea and sugar and meal weekly up to 2/6, and some bedclothes.

1859 *I. was in such a state of filth no-one would receive him in their house. He would need a pair of drawers, socks, shirt, moleskin trousers and jacket. His clothes, crawling with vermin, would require to be burnt.*

The government passed a new law, in 1845, to help the very poor who were too young, old or ill to work. But it did not agree to help people fit to work who could not find a job, **B**. The Parochial Boards noted down important decisions they made. **C** includes several of these minutes from just one of Scotland's Boards.

D

Name	Age	Offence	Punishment
James T.	6	Choking drain with stones and turning off water. *Remarks* Continually in mischief. Breakfast an hour late as a result of water being turned off.	4 strokes on the buttocks with cane.
Elspeth G.	30	Using bad language. Ill-treating her child. Bringing in whisky. Refusing to work.	Porridge milk stopped for 2 days.
Joseph C.	77	Leaving the House without leave, attempting to strike with a stick, threatening to stab the Assistant Governor.	10 hours confinement in the cell.

Sometimes the Boards joined together and built special poorhouses where poor people had to live if they expected help. **D** is a picture of one of these places, the Kincardine Poorhouse at Stonehaven. By 1895 there were 66 poorhouses in Scotland. Most of them were run very strictly and people who broke the poorhouse rules were punished, **E**.

Most poor people lived in their own homes, in lodgings, or with their families. People who were very poor because they simply could not find jobs suffered a great deal. They did not have a right to any help at all, but sometimes committees were set up to help them:

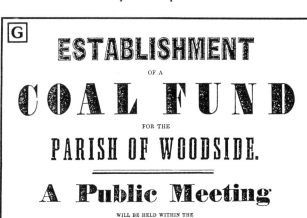

G

ESTABLISHMENT

OF A

COAL FUND

FOR THE

PARISH OF WOODSIDE.

A Public Meeting

WILL BE HELD WITHIN THE

SESSION-HOUSE OF **WOODSIDE**,

On Wednesday, Nov. 18,

For the purpose of Establishing a Fund to provide COALS for the destitute Poor of the Parish in the winter season.

CHAIR TO BE TAKEN AT HALF-PAST TWO, P.M., PRECISELY.

The attendance of the Heritors, Householders, and the benevolent generally, connected with the locality, is earnestly requested.

F *A man calling on the poor on the day of a blizzard reports that in 40 houses there was not one spark of fire. The local committees for the relief of the poor with soup and coal have been at work. On certain days they are willing to sell as much soup for a penny as will make a warm dinner for 6.* The Fraserburgh Herald, December 1885

G is a further clue to how these poor were helped.

? ? ? ? ? ? ? ? ? ? ? ? ?

1 Use **A** to answer the following:
a Which group of people collected money to give the poor?
b Which poor people wore badges?
c What sort of food did the poor eat?
d Why were poor people very likely to be ill?
e How did some poor people solve the problem of their miserable lives in Scotland?

2 Many of the witnesses who gave the evidence in **A** were doctors and church ministers. Why would they know about the poor?

3 Look at **E**. Work out from this what the rules and punishments were in this poorhouse. Write out the rules and punishments as a list to be pinned up there. Put the name of the poorhouse at the top.

4 **G** is a poster. Design a similar poster for the soup kitchen mentioned in **F**.

A HEALTHY LIFE?

If your family's doctor visits your home to see one of the family who is ill do you have to pay him? During the nineteenth century people had to pay to see doctors. In **A** you can see how much Inverness doctors charged. An ordinary person probably earned a pound a week, perhaps less. Yet people needed treatment even more than today. Terrible diseases were common, diseases that are rare today.

Newspapers were full of advertisements like **B**, but many of these medicines were useless. In the early nineteenth century doctors did not under-stand why many illnesses happened. Their cures often concentrated on making patients bleed or be sick.

People were most frightened of a disease called cholera. It spread through dirty water. Thousands died in outbreaks in 1832, 1848 and 1852. When cholera came to a town or village the people there were filled with fear:

C *On my arrival at Collieston the excitement and alarm were extreme. All work was stopped. The villagers had been prevented by the authorities from entering neighbouring towns with fish for sale . . . . The sound of the funeral bell, the death of a relation or neighbour produced extreme excitement and alarm.*

Until the later nineteenth century, doctors did not understand how cholera spread. The authorities gave people advice that was often very little use:

D *The Provost and Magistrates of Elgin earnestly recommended the following regulations in the event of Cholera appearing:*

— Strict attention to personal cleanliness, to cleanliness of Dwelling Houses, to Warm Clothing, to regular hours of Sleep, to keeping indoors at night and taking food before going out in the morning, may be relied upon.

— The Board are providing that should the

A **Medical fees in Inverness, 1818**

	Rich person	Poor person
A single visit in the day	10/6	2/6
" " " " " night	£1. 1/-	5/-
Country visit up to 4 miles	£2. 2/-	10/6
Consultation by letter	£1. 1/-	
Surgery charges –		
An amputation (arm or leg off)	£21. --	£2. 2/-
Extracting teeth	£1.1/-	2/6
Delivering child	£10.10/-	£1. 1/-

E Improvements in Scottish Health

1800	Vaccination against smallpox was being quite widely used.
1845	As part of the change in the poor law, the government offered money to persuade the new parochial boards to pay doctors to care for the poor.
1847	Dr Simpson in Edinburgh developed the use of chloroform to put patients to sleep during operations. (Earlier, patients were usually made drunk.)
1860	Joseph Lister in Edinburgh began to use carbolic sprays and dressings to stop wounds caused by operations becoming infected.
1864	Smallpox vaccination was made compulsory.
1867	The new Public Health Act gave local authorities more power to make towns and cities cleaner and healthier.
1889	Scottish universities allowed women to train as doctors.

disease appear several Hospitals shall be opened.

— *The Board recommend Mustard Poultices, and Hot Air Baths.*

— *The Board think that blood letting has been very generally found useful.*

— *In addition the Provost and Magistrates recommend that rollers of Flannel be worn, about 6 to 8 inches broad, to be rolled twice round the body, above the hips.*

Health care improved partly because authorities began to improve living conditions and partly because doctors came to understand the causes of several illnesses. **E** shows some of the improvements in health care in the nineteenth century. Many of Britain's doctors trained in Scotland. Between 1800 and 1850, 8000 of 8291 doctors who qualified came from Scotland. In 1832 a law allowed those teaching doctors to cut up the bodies of poor people (if no one claimed them for burial). Until then, grave-robbers had stolen bodies and sold them to doctors. In the graveyards of old churches you can often see little watchhouses used by relatives guarding bodies that had just been buried. In Edinburgh two Irishmen, William Burke and William Hare decided to murder people in order to sell the bodies to a famous teacher, Robert Knox. They were finally caught in 1828. **F** is a newspaper report on the murder of Mary Paterson:

F *She was murdered in Burke's brother's house in the Canongate by Burke and Hare. She was put into a teabox and carried to Dr*

Knox's dissecting rooms and (they) got £8 for her body.

When they first began this murdering system they always took them to Knox's after dark: but being so successful they went in the day time and grew more bold. They often said that no person could find them out. They made it their business to decoy persons into their houses to murder them.

Many hospitals were built in the later nineteenth century. The doctors working in them were better trained. But notice in **G** that they are operating wearing ordinary clothes. Nursing care improved too. By 1900 big hospitals had well organized wards run by properly qualified matrons.

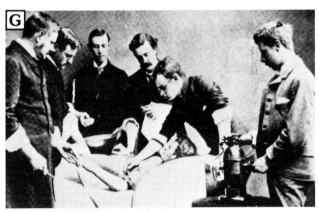

An operating theatre in 1869

??????????????

1 Complete these sentences:
  a Cholera spread from drinking dirty _____.
  b _____ was the first person to use carbolic sprays.
  c After 1847 hospitals used _____ to put patients to sleep before operating.
  d Vaccination for smallpox was compulsory after _____.

2 Cholera Panic! You are the Provost of a town where a cholera case has just been found. Design a bold simple poster (using **D**), to advise people how to behave.

3 How different are hospital scenes today from the one in **G**? List as many differences as possible.

4 One of the murderers in **F** confessed his crimes. He was William Hare. Write 'My confession', as if written by Hare.

IMPROVING CONDITIONS

During the nineteenth century people crowded into Scotland's towns and cities. More and more people went to work in factories, mines and workshops. You have already read about some of the problems that this caused. The government decided it would have to do something about some of these problems. It passed many laws **A**.

Ordinary people began to see their lives improve. The people in charge of towns, cities and the countryside gradually got the power and the money to make Scotland a pleasanter place in which to live. Officials travelled about the country checking whether new laws were being obeyed:

B *I find there are at least 41 piggeries with*

1833 Burgh Reform Act: The governments of towns and cities were improved and given more power to carry out improvements.
1833 Factory Act: Children under 9 not to work in cotton mills: 9 to 13 year olds to work no more than 8 hours a day.
1842 Mines Act: Females and boys under 10 were no longer allowed to work underground in mines.
1844 Factory Act: Children of 8 to 13 to work no more than a 6½ hour day.
1845 Poor Law Reform: Very poor people unable to work to be looked after by their local 'Parochial Board'. The Board could use locally collected money.
1847 Ten Hours Act: Under 18s and all women to work no more than 10 hours a day.
1862 Burgh Reform Act: Places with a population of 700 able to get power to greatly improve their living conditions.
1867 Public Health Act: Cities and towns given much more power to clean streets, lay sewers, provide safe water and build hospitals.
1872 Education Act: All children between 5 and 13 to go to school. School Boards to set up satisfactory schools.
1889 Local Government Reform: Country areas to be much better organized with elected County Councils and District Councils.

ADVERTISEMENTS. [WORRALL'S

ABERDEEN

PIG REARING ESTABLISHMENT,
FOUNTAINHALL HOUSE, ABERDEEN,
A. M. GRAY, PROPRIETOR.

YOUNG PIGS, HALF-GROWN PIGS,
AND BREEDING SOWS.

ALSO

Pure Essex & Berkshire's, & First Crosses from those Celebrated Breeds.
ALL ORDERS BOOKED AND DELIVERED IN STRICT ROTATION.

about 105 pigs. Generally I have found them in bad order, ruinous, some too near houses, some are in Gardens, barrels and boxes being used for the Pigstyes, with dirty puddles in winter and a smell in summer.
The Report of an Inspector of Works, Fraserburgh, 1892.

C *Water is obtained from 120 wells. They are either in backyards or near middens and dung-heaps. The use of these waters is dangerous to health. Slaughterhouses were too close to homes and had piggeries into which blood escaped and offal was thrown.*
Report on Inverurie, 1874, by a doctor sent from Edinburgh to inspect the burgh.

Scotland's towns and cities were unhealthy places. People lived crowded together, and so did animals like hens, ducks and pigs, **D**. The officials in charge of tackling town problems were called 'Police Commissioners'. They tried to improve the health, safety and appearance of their towns. **E** shows some of the problems and decisions dealt with by the Police Commissioners in just one town. All over Scotland other officials were trying to solve similar difficulties. The improved state of Scottish towns today owes much to the work of these Victorian people. It also owes a great deal to the work of the humble scavengers who cleaned the towns. The rules in **F** were drawn up in mid Victorian times to guide the scavengers of Aberdeen. **G** shows a *scaffie* or scavenger who worked in Inverurie.

E Fraserburgh Police Commissioners' Minutes

1840 First meeting. A shilling rate to be gathered.

1841 Gaslighting to be introduced. Two lamplighters appointed.

1848 Estimates needed from wrights and painters for 3 inch letters painted white on black background, for street names.
Street scavengers to be employed.

1850 Pavements to be laid in Broad Street.

1851 Ditches to be cut to connect new spring water to a fountain.
A new water reservoir to be built.

1859 A public privy (toilet) to be placed by School Park.

1860 Contractors needed to cart dung. The contractors shall be bound every Tuesday, Thursday and Saturday between the hours of 6 am and 10 am to cart away the whole dung that may have been collected in heaps by the scavengers, to the dung depot.

1866 Pigsties kept in a filthy condition are a nuisance, fowls living on the streets are a nuisance, all ducks are especially a nuisance and must be removed.

1868 A twenty shilling fine or 10 days prison for
- every person who throws dirt, dirty water, ashes, nightsoil on the street
- people who put dung on the street 10 am to 11 pm
- owners of ferocious dogs allowed to wander
- people who drive wagons and don't keep to the left
- people keeping pigsties next to the street without a proper wall.

1871 A watering trough to be provided.

1872 A Fire Brigade to be set up.

1873 Ashpits are full, drains choked, the channels in many of the streets in a bad state.

1875 A general scheme of laying sewers is to be adopted.

F Rules for the Aberdeen scavengers

1 Each man must be at his place at 4 o'clock in the morning.

2 The squads will clean out ashpits, cesspools and privies and have their contents removed by carts.

3 Streets and lanes will be swept.

4 An hour will be allowed for breakfast from 9 to 10.

5 A note must be kept of the names of persons who make a practice of throwing out filth.

6 There will be an hour for dinner. Scavengers will leave work at 4.0. The usual hour for leaving work on Saturday will be 5 o'clock. They shall give their services on Sunday morning from 7.0 to 9.0

7 Each man is to be sober and steady, civil and obliging to the public.

G

???????????????

1 Imagine you are an elderly street scavenger like the Inverurie scaffie in **G**. Use the evidence to tell your young grandson about how life in your town has changed. Mention:

a what sort of work you do and the hours you work

b what a mess the town used to be in

c new laws and the Police Commissioners

d some of the changes you have seen take place in lighting, paving, cleaning, getting fresh water etc.

2 Look at the 1868 entry in **E**. Design a notice to be put up by the Police Commissioners warning people of offences for which they will be punished. Do you think others should be added?

THE NEW POLICE

Law and order in early nineteenth century Scotland was enforced by part-time constables and by badly paid (and often elderly) night-watchmen. But as the country's population grew, towns and cities expanded and it was hard for these people to deal with criminals. From the 1830s Scotland began to copy the full-time police service Sir Robert Peel had set up in London. **A** shows the kind of work these early policemen carried out. **B** shows some of the crimes that policemen tackled. The police wore dark blue uniforms and carried staffs **C**. Some people were suspicious of the police, but others welcomed them. In 1842 the minister of the Aberdeenshire town of Turriff wrote:

D *One of the most crying evils was the overwhelming concourse (gathering) of*

B **Crimes in Elgin, March & April 1849**

Assault	39
Begging	17
Boys riding on the back of coaches	7
Drunk and disorderly	26
Drunk and furious driving	4
Drunk and breaking windows	1
Chimney on fire	3
Exposing unwholesome meat for sale	2
Firing squibs in streets	2
Hawking (selling) without licence	6
Theft	24
Firing guns	3
Fraud	17

A **Regulations for Elgin Police 1836**

1 There shall be one principal police officer at £20 with uniform, hat and coat.
2 There shall be one assistant police officer at £12 with uniform, hat and coat.
3 The first duty of the principal officer every morning 6 to 7 am in summer, and daybreak in winter − to visit such low tippling and boarding houses known to be the resort of vagrants and loose characters and shall convey out of the town all vagrants (wandering beggars).
4 The officer shall go round the town at least 5 times a day and shall be at all times ready to act when called upon to suppress riots and take up thieves.
5 The officer shall remove from the streets all obstructions to free passage and prevent furious and irregular driving of carriages and carts or rolling of wheelbarrows or carrying unwieldy burdens on the side passages.
6 On market days and on occasions of popular excitement and of an unusually crowded state of the town, both officers shall parade the streets from 8.0 am to 10.0 pm and be ready to act even during the night if called upon. They will be provided with batons which are to be used principally in self defence.
7 The officers are debarred from receiving gratuities (gifts) in money.

vagrants who made this place a favourite haven. Since the institution of the police and the activities of the district constable with the terror which his baton and uniform inspire, this annoyance has been much lessened. In this locality, therefore, though a feeling of opposition has been shown in some quarters, the general desire is that the force be kept.

Policemen were paid the same sort of wages as ordinary working men. But they were expected to behave very well. Most men drank a great deal of beer and public houses were open all day. The authorities in Elgin (in N.E. Scotland) noted, in 1842:

E *The meeting considered the case of an officer who had been the worse for liquor whilst on duty. He confessed his fault but being his first offence trusted the Board would forgive him on promise of better behaviour in future.*

There were many cases like this.

Police forces in big cities included detectives. One of the most famous of Victorian detectives worked in Edinburgh in the 1850s. His name was James McLevy. These are some extracts from his casebook:

F *I can always tell an unlucky thief from a lucky one, one with full fobs from one with empty pockets, one who suspects being scented from one who is on the scent.*

He thought his success was due to careful observation:

People give McLevy praise for some extraordinary powers. It is all nonsense. My deductions have been, and are, very simple pieces of business.

The Bridewell prison, Aberdeen

G

He spent a lot of time wandering around the places that he knew criminals went to. At certain public houses and lodging houses he often found stolen goods. He wrote that:

Among these there was the 'Cock and Trumpet'. On one occasion I issued triumphantly with a cheese weighing 30 pounds, on another with a dozen sausages and on another with 2 live geese. The landlady never knew that such things were in her house.

One thief he found, with stolen hens and ducks, *'plucking lustily at the fowls.'* He had finished nine hens and was busy with the last of nine ducks. *'What a fine show of poultry, Sandy now'* said I, *'Where got you so many hens and ducks?'* Replied the rogue, *'They flew in at the window'.*

McLevy knew many criminals by sight. For years he had been trying to catch a thief called Adam McDonald. One day he saw him, with a friend called Chisholm, taking a drunk called Kerr down a dark alley. He remembered what happened with pleasure.

In an instant the feet were taken from Kerr, he was thrown flat on his back with a sound of his head on the granite. Chisholm held him down, Adam whirling his gold chain over the victim's head, rolled it up in his hand along with the watch and bolted. But whither did Adam bolt? Into my very arms! He commenced to struggle with me which, if I had not been of the strength I am would have ended in his escape, while spluttering, 'McLevy! The devil of all devils!'

Convicted criminals might be sent to a prison like **G**.

? ? ? ? ? ? ? ? ? ? ? ?

1 Whose idea for a police service did Scotland copy?

2 What did police carry as weapons?

3 Look at **A** and **B**. Imagine you are one of Elgin's early policemen. Write a report for the people in charge of you to describe how you have spent your day. Mention your hours of duty, how you spent the time and the crimes that you dealt with.

4 Look at **F**. What was it that made McLevy such a good detective?

HERRING FISHING

A shows a boat of the 1900s fishing for herring. During the nineteenth century Scotland's herring fisheries grew very rapidly and the boats increased in size B. The government helped the industry with extra money paid for good quality catches. Herring provided food for the growing population as well as exports to Eastern European lands where it was very popular. The fisheries provided work for thousands of men and women.

A Fishing for herring

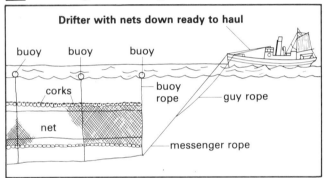

Drifter with nets down ready to haul

buoy   buoy   buoy

corks

buoy rope

guy rope

net

messenger rope

B Herring boats of the nineteenth century

	cost	length
SKAFFIE, built from 1800 onwards	£50–£100	25 to 30 feet
ZULU, built from 1879	£500–£800	50 to 60 feet
STEAM DRIFTER built from 1880	£1500–£3000	60 to 85 feet

C shows fishing boats anchored in Fraserburgh harbour whilst the men stow the cotton nets (there is a 'Zulu' type vessel in the foreground). In the 1860s cotton replaced hemp in net making. Because of cotton's lighter weight boats could carry twice the number of nets once it was introduced. The boats put to sea in late afternoon, sailed up to 50 miles and fished through the night. The herring season began off Lewis and Shetland in May, reached Aberdeenshire in July and continued down to East Anglia in autumn.

HERRING BOATS, FRASERBURGH. 13,071. G.W.W.

William Leiper lived in a fisher cottage a hundred years ago:

D *Our cottage consisted of a but and ben and a dark loft for nets and lines. The two rooms each had a fireplace. Our food consisted of porridge and milk in the morning; potatoes, fish from the store barrel at midday, and soup or oatcakes in the evening.*

As the fishing fleets worked their way round the coast, following the shoals of herring, a large number of girls and women accompanied them on land. They prepared the herring once it had been landed **E**. Jean Bochel remembered her life as a fisher girl

F *Usually the foreman came and knocked at every door at 5 o'clock. 'Get up, get up.' If it was your day on ye had tae get up and light the fire and boil the kettle, make a cup of tea and bread and butter. And then we started work at six prompt. We had oilskin skirts and we had kerchiefs on our heads and we tied our fingers with cotton cloths. We gutted and packed three barrels in an hour. By the time they were filled up there were a thousand herring in the barrel.*

The girls worked till 10 pm after a big catch had been landed. They worked in teams of three, two to gut and one to pack the herring in barrels of salt. A team shared about eight pence for every barrel they filled. The girls stayed in huts and sheds in fishertowns like Wick and Fraserburgh. Life was very hard:

G *Ye'd tae take in water in pails from an outside tap and put on pans of water on tae a coal fire. And washing facilities – we'd a barrel o' rain water and a basin.*

H *We took our own beds wi us – chaff! And our own cooking utensils. No electric oven, nor gas cookers nor nothin, just the open fire.*

Their living conditions were often very miserable. In 1890 Georgina Robertson reported:

J *. . . many of the girls' rooms unfit for human habitation – smoky, dirty, draughty, without cupboards or shelves and only one bedstead to every 3 girls. The girls have to live, cook and wash as well as sleep in the space, in many cases it is insufficient. But the most crying evil is the want of WCs near the lodgings and in the*

E

Women gutting herring on the quayside at Fraserburgh

curing yards, consequently the beach and outskirts of the town are in a disgusting condition. There have been many ailments among the fisher folk arising from the want of these conveniences. They said they were treated like Beasts.

? ? ? ? ? ? ? ? ? ? ? ?

1 The foreground vessel in **C** shows the size of a Zulu's crew. How many were in the crew? There is also a clue to how the men hauled in nets full of fish. What is it?

2 The cotton nets of the 1860s meant bigger catches were gathered. Look at **B** to find a second reason why more herring were caught in the later nineteenth century.

3 Look at **B**. Why might some fishermen prefer a Zulu to a steam drifter? Suggest an *advantage* the steam drifter might have had over a Zulu.

4 Imagine you ar a 14-year-old girl on her first year's fish work. Write a letter home describing the conditions in which you live and the work that you do.

THE VANISHING CROFTERS

A

In many places in the Highlands and Islands you can see ruined buildings like those in **A**. Who once lived here? Why did they leave?

We can answer these questions by looking at the pictures and writings of the past. The people who once lived here farmed tiny plots of land called *crofts*. They lived in very simple homes.

B *It consists of a butt, a benn and a byre* (that is a kitchen, inner room and a place to put cattle). *In the centre of the butt is heaped up dirt and stones in which is fixed small iron bars, leaving a hollow as a grate* (for fire): *there is also a crank that moves any way to which is hooked the pot* (for cooking). *There is no chimney but a hole* (in the roof). *The dirt floor is full of holes retaining wet or dirt. In one corner is a box nailed to the partition between the butt and benn with a door in front in which is a bed with a great many blankets. Into this box creep as many as it can hold. In this house stood another box containing milk, oatcakes, broth etc. and eating utensils.*

The dunghill is close to the door of the house. Next to the dunghill stand their peat stacks. In places the substitute for candles are the stumps of trees.

C shows a Highland couple outside their blackhouse.

About 200 years ago many Highland landlords began to force crofters to leave their homes. Some of the ruined buildings of today are the result of these events. In 1854 a scientist visiting the West of Scotland saw a group of crofters being cleared from their homes. He wrote:

D *One of the most vivid memories I retain is of the clearance of the crofts of Suishnish. (The landlords')* main aim was to make as much money as possible; they decided to clear out the whole population and convert the ground into one large sheep farm.

One afternoon a strange wailing sound reached my ears. I could see a long procession winding along the road. There were old men and women too feeble to walk who were placed in carts, the younger ones carrying their bundles of clothes and household goods, while the children walked alongside. Everyone was in tears. The people were on their way to be shipped to Canada. Not a soul is to be seen there now but the crumbling walls mark where a community once lived.

Some landowners turned much of their estates into large sheep farms **E**. They wanted the crofters' land for sheep. Many homes were then burned to stop people trying to return.

Some landlords provided new homes for crofters in villages on the coast. Others helped Highlanders go abroad to live. Many of those who were able to cling on to their crofts found it hard to survive. Their main food was potatoes and if the crop failed, people starved. This letter came from a group of 600 people, in 1850:

F *We have to tell you that our potatoes have almost entirely failed and many of us and our*

E **The increase in sheep farming 1800 – 55**

Number of sheep in Sutherland:	15 000 in 1811
	204 000 in 1855
Number of sheep in Inverness County:	50 000 in 1800
	588 000 in 1855
Number of sheep in Argyllshire:	278 000 in 1800
	827 000 in 1855

children will suffer severely during the next winter unless some food is offered to us. We are very ill off for clothing and we know not what to do. We are on the brink of starvation.

Crofters who left farming because life was so hard were joined in the towns and cities by others who had been forced to leave. In the later nineteenth century clearances continued. Landlords began to turn out crofters to make great game reserves in which animals could be hunted. But the crofters began to resist. In 1886 the government passed a new law making life a little easier for surviving crofters.

C

? ? ? ? ? ? ? ? ? ? ? ?

1 Using **B** and the extra detail of house shapes in **C** draw a plan of a Highland home, showing the detail of the fireplace, box bed, the dunghill and the peat stack.

2 From all the clues in this section why do you think that:

    a the house roof in **C** is held down with stones?

    b the people in **B** slept in a large box, crowded together?

    c many landlords preferred sheep on their lands to people?

    d the people in **F** were starving instead of buying food?

3 Imagine you are a policeman who has been helping to turn out a family. Write a report for your inspector. Describe how a landlord's agent came to ask for your help, how you felt as the people were ordered out, what the agent said to explain why the landowner needed the land and what the people said about how they felt and what they thought their future might be.

THE TOURISTS' HIGHLANDS

The Highlands became a popular holiday area in the later nineteenth century. Queen Victoria helped to bring this about. **A** is part of the journal she kept. It shows some of the reasons why rich people liked the Highlands.

A *Ben Lomond, blue and yellow, rose above the lower hills which were pink and purple with heather. We got out and sketched. Only here and there were some poor little cottages with picturesque barefooted lasses and children to be seen.*

During the whole of our drive nothing could be quieter or more agreeable. Hardly a creature did we meet. The solitude, the romance and wild loneliness of everything here, the independent simple people who all speak Gaelic all make beloved Scotland the proudest finest country in the world.

Victoria and her husband Prince Albert spent many months at Balmoral. The home they had built there was made to look like a castle. **B** gives a glimpse of the Queen, with her guests, outside Balmoral. Rich people enjoyed shooting birds and deer **C**. They altered large parts of the Highlands to suit the creatures they liked to hunt. But other sorts of tourists came too:

D *Deeside teems with visitors, tourists, sportsmen, cyclists and mountaineers of every grade, from the prince of royal blood who delights in deer-stalking to the humblest city worker who has to content himself with the trout fishing or rambling of a single annual holiday.*

The Queen's presence at Balmoral made this area very popular. Her arrival at nearby Ballater Station was a great event, as Amy Stewart Fraser remembers

E *How well I remember the days when Queen Victoria used to arrive in the royal train at Ballater. She drove off in an open carriage. Throughout the long years of her summer-into-autumn residence at Balmoral her arrival never failed to attract a loyal cheering crowd. Beside the top-hatted coachman sat a liveried footman and 2 others stood on a ledge behind the Queen.*

Many tourists stayed at the hotels which were built in Victorian times **F**. The arrival of large numbers of visitors altered the area. But not everyone welcomed the change, like Christian Watt, who came to Deeside in the mid nineteenth century selling fish:

B

A Victorian shooting party

G *The folks on the upper reaches of the Dee spoke the Gaelic. They lived to awful long ages. The smell of the hills and the air was so wonderful, at night the whole valley was filled with the sound of bagpipes. This was long before the Queen came. After Royalty came Deeside was ruined. The rich came and built huge palaces to try and outshine Balmoral. In our fisher dress a group of us stood by the roadside near Crathie. The Queen came by, she looked so sour you could have hung a jug on her mouth. The wide area was now invaded by the curious. Our hill trade was ruined for we were no longer permitted to cross the mountains after they made the deer forests.*

Victoria probably had little idea when she wrote **H** what the people who watched her were really thinking.

H *An old fish wife with her creel on her back, bare legs and feet and very short petticoat began waving a handkerchief and almost dancing as we drove away. Brown (Victoria's servant) motioned to her to come on and threw her something which the poor old thing ran to pick up.*

? ? ? ? ? ? ? ? ? ? ? ?

It is not easy to say whether or not the coming of tourists helped the Highlands. Use all the evidence here to list as many reasons as you can find

a to suggest tourists helped the Highlands

b to suggest tourists harmed the Highlands.

What do you think? Add your own ideas.

A DAY OUT, 1888

A hundred years ago Scottish people enjoyed going out just as people do today. They went shopping. They ate in cafes. They went to all sorts of entertainments. The information on these pages comes from magazines for the year 1888 that were on sale in Aberdeen. The magazines used drawings, not photographs, to brighten up their pages. They show some of the entertainments Aberdeen people could go to.

1 Look through the advertisements to find and describe:

a the kind of bicycle used in cycle races.

b the kind of clothes worn by lady bathers.

c an entertainment you would not expect to be able to see today.

d a moving hut for bathers to change in.

2 Which entertainment would you have chosen to go to? Give reasons for your answer.

3 Search through modern newspapers and magazines and make up a similar display of advertisements. What is present in your display that was not there 100 years ago?

If your school is near to a large library you should be able to find advertisements showing the sort of entertainments available 100 years ago in your area.

A MODERN TRAGEDY.

BOTH ENDS OF THE MACHINE

THE GREAT WAR

Between 1914 and 1918 Britain and France fought a war against Germany. Thousands of Scotsmen died in this war. Today, every Scottish town and village contains a war memorial like **A**.

At first many men welcomed the war as an adventure. Murdo Maclennan recalls how he joined a cavalry unit:

B *The men that were in those days in the Scouts were outstanding. Strong men, tremendous men. I joined the Lovat Scouts in 1911. And at that time you had to provide your own horse. We went away to the war. The war was to be over in 6 months. Everybody was anxious to get to the war — back in 6 months. But it was a long 6 months!*

Men like Murdo were encouraged to join the army by government posters like **C**. But the Great War took place in miserable conditions. A former pupil of Milne's Institute, Fochabers,

wrote to tell the school about going up to the battle front:

D *We set off in single file for the entrance trenches and crept along quietly. We were startled by the whizz of shells coming towards us. 'Down you go, we've been spotted' came the order. After a considerable time had passed I waited for the man in front of me to get up and move on. I nudged him. He did not move so I nudged him again. Turning him round I saw with a shudder that I had laid down behind a dead man. We now had to creep on our hands and knees, slipping in the mud.*

When the time came to attack the men had to clamber out of their trenches and rush forward, **E**. This was called 'going over the top':

F *Before you went in you were frightened. But after you got mucked in the fear sort of left you. Sometimes conditions were so bad you didn't care whether you were shot or not. When the whistle blew you just went over the top and ran like steam through the barbed wire and into the other fellow's trench and went at it hand to hand. Rifle and bayonet.*

E

Between attacks the soldiers sheltered in 'dug-outs' in the trenches, **G**.

The war consisted of numerous terrible battles. It ended in November 1918 with German defeat. An officer in a Scottish regiment described memories that stayed in his mind for the rest of his life:

H *Incidents flash through the memory: the battles of the first 4 months; the awful winters in waterlogged trenches, cold and miserable; the terrible trench-war attacks and shell fire of the next 3 years; loss of friends, exhaustion and wounds; the victories of the last few months; all our enemies beaten. Thank God! The end of 4 dreadful years.*

As Murdo Maclennan pointed out, the war cost the lives of far too many men:

J *Oh the country was bled white. Where I come from there were 7 young men killed out of a total population of 100. It was the same all over the Highlands.*

The war memorial in the place where you live will tell you how many local people died in the Great War.

G

???????????

1 Using **G**, describe what a trench was like.

2 Do you think **C** was likely to persuade men to join up? Give a reason for your answer.

3 From **F**, how was the order given to climb out of the trenches to attack?

4 What obstacle lay between attackers and the enemy trenches?

5 Write a short story called 'The Nightmare'. A former soldier wakes in the night because he has been dreaming about the Great War in which he once fought. He tells his wife about his dream.

6 Find your local war memorial. What does it tell you about World War I?

THE GREAT WAR: AT HOME

A

Soldiers' families waited for news. It often came scribbled on the back of postcards like **A**. How does this view of the war compare with the evidence in the previous section? Families sent back presents to the men at the front. From **B** you can work out some of the sorts of things they sent.

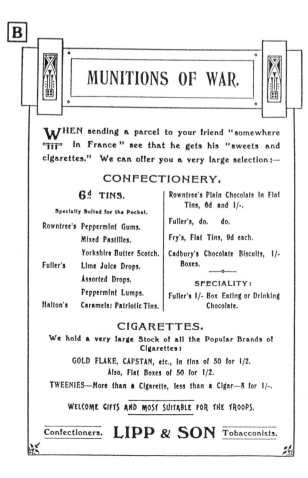

So many men joined the armed forces that women had to begin to take over the jobs men had once done. A girl describes how she left home and finished up in a munitions factory:

C *I was born in the village of North Tolsta in the Isle of Lewis and I was still very young when our country was first at war with Germany. After that there was an urgent call for female workers for the jute factories in Dundee. I, along with six others, answered the call. Then I volunteered for munitions and I was called up and worked in an explosives factory. I lived in a Government Hostel. I know I had no money sense, it was just a question of helping my country.*

One of the biggest of these factories was in Gretna on the border with England. The women lived in special hostels. **D** shows the jobs they had left. The Government tried to organize their lives strictly:

E *To keep the workers in the factory area and away from temptations elsewhere, no late evening trains were run between Carlisle and Gretna except on Saturday when the latest train left at 9.30 pm.*

Women police, **F**, kept the workers in order, indeed it was the war that led to the setting up of a women's police force.

The war showed women were well able to do many jobs once only carried out by men. Margaret Morrison was 22 when she left home for a better-paid job than she had ever imagined she would get.

G *I'd worked as a laundry maid. Most of us had never worked on machines before. We*

D The former jobs of the 11000 women at the Gretna hostel were:
 Domestic servants 36%
 Living at home, no job 20%
 Other munition works 15%
 Ordinary factory workers 12%
 Shop assistants 5%
 Laundry workers, farm workers, dressmakers, teachers, clerks 12%

were given a week's instruction. After a while they said we could do as well as any of the skilled workmen. Of course we didn't get the same pay. We worked a 12 hour shift but the pay was good.

Even children helped. **H** comes from a 1915 magazine produced by a Fochabers school.

H *The pupils have been doing what they could for our soldiers and sailors, making scarves, pillow cases etc. for the comfort of the men. They have also given freely of their pennies. On Empire Day the pupils were asked to contribute a little to send to our own old pupils in the fighting line some tobacco, sweets etc. Two classes at a time bring in a collection of flowers on Thursday morning. They are packed in boxes and sent to hospital ships at Cromarty and Queensferry.*

The end of the war came as a great relief to families who feared for the safety of their men-folk. Charlotte Roncone's mother was so excited she trudged miles to join in the celebrations:

J *I'll never know what possessed my mother to walk the 3½ miles to Dundee on Armistice Day, pushing a baby in the big boat-shaped pram with a child hanging on each side; but I do remember the excitement of the thronging masses.*

There was a declaration read out from the Town Hall and there were pipe bands and brass bands. I remember the terror when, in the surging crowds, I was swept away. A young kilted Black Watch soldier lifted me onto his shoulders. *He took command, battled his way to Macdonald's Restaurant, and appealed to the diners to squeeze up for a soldier and his family. My sister demanded 'Are you really my daddy?': At six years she had seen very little of our father.*

The war changed women's lives in many ways. At its end they at last got the right to vote in Parliamentary elections.

??????????????

1 Look at **A**.
a Is there anything here you think is reliable evidence of what trench life was like?
b List any points that you think give a misleading picture of trench life.
c Why would the Government not allow postcards with pictures like the one in the previous section?
d Do you think soldiers would be allowed to write what they wanted on the back of the cards?
e Do you think the Government was right to try and control what people read and heard about the war?

2 From the evidence in **C**, **D**, **E** and **G** do you think the war changed women's lives for the better? Give reasons for your answer.

3 Imagine you are a soldier at the front and write a postcard to your family. Mention presents you have received. (Look at **B** and **H** for ideas for this.)

47

THE GENERAL STRIKE OF 1926

Alex Warrender was a coal miner. He lived in East Fife. Yet one day in May 1926, instead of being at work, he was helping to attack a lorry.

A *Well a beer lorry came frae, I think it was Youngers o' Alloa making for St Andrews. And when it got the length o' Muiredge it turned to come doon the Wellesley road. It was stopped and telled to turn back, and he refused. So they couped (overturned) the lorry. Of course barrels o' beer was burst open and it was runnin' on the pavements and somebody went for the police and there were about 20 or 30 police come up in nae time. Several people was arrested and the rest, me included, we ran oot the road.*

What caused this event?

Scotland contains several coal fields, including the one in East Fife (see the map on page 64). After the Great War the price of Scottish coal was sharply cut: other countries produced cheaper coal. Mine owners tried to save money by lowering miners' wages. But miners worked at a hard and dangerous job. **B** shows that they still used simple tools. There were too few modern machines in Scottish pits. The miners belonged to a union called the Miners Federation. In 1926 they went on strike to protest against the pay cuts.

Other trade unions throughout Britain supported the miners. From 4 to 12 May they joined in the General Strike. Bill Ballantyne was a railwayman. He remembered how Scottish trade unionists joined the strike:

C *We had, in Scotland, brought road and rail transport to a stop. At least in the areas that mattered.*

The government used volunteers (especially students) to try and run the railways. Bill Ballantyne and his fellow workers tried to stop them:

D *We soon put an end to that nonsense. We knew where the steep slopes were so we greased the rails. When the engine came on to the greasy bit it just stood and danced: it couldn't get a grip and they didn't know how to handle it.*

The government used soldiers and police too. It was, as Bill knew, a critical time:

E *I realised it was more than a battle for the miners. This was a challenge to pin us (workers) down, slash our wages, and in the case of the miners, increase our hours. I didn't see it as a revolutionary challenge but I felt it must be a challenge to the Government.*

The trade unions were not well prepared. They did not have much money. On 9 May all unions except the miners went back to work. But the miners stayed out for seven months. In Fife, as in other areas, hunger began to force men back to work. Alex Warrender thought that men who went back were wrong to do so:

F *Well as the Strike wore on and there was no sign of the miners gonna get the benefit of it, some people wanted to get back to work. A few of them belonging to this district got up in the morning and awa' to the pit. After a day or twa it was noticed so they decided to put pickets on. I believe some of them got a bit of a doing afore the police were brought in to escort them. They maybe had a job but they never had nae friends during that time.*

Two of his fellow miners remember how they managed to keep going even though they had no wages:

G *The soup kitchen was a godsend. Well you was lucky if you got a plate o' soup and maybe a mashed potato or a bit o' corned beef. That's a' that could be afforded.*

H *I've seen me comin' in wi' maybe 8 or 10 rabbits. I used tae do a bit o' fishin' tae. People a' helped one anither. As far as the boots was concerned I used tae go along the beach tae the rubbish bins. I'd gather old boots, dismantle them and take off them what would be serviceable for us.*

Eventually the miners gave way. The mine owners cut their wages and wouldn't give work to strike leaders like William Murray:

J *After the General Strike I was unable to get work of any description at all. I went round the pits. I went to the builders and other employers in Leven but whenever my name was known that was me out. I was without work for 6 to 7 years. Fortunately after that I was employed by Leven Town Council.*

K *The Aberdeen Press & Journal, 4th May 1926.*
No one who approached the question with a calm mind can fail to rally to the government's assistance and do his or her utmost to see that this menace to liberty and prosperity will be swiftly crushed. There never has been such an exhibition of madness, working men, in forming the T.U.C., have fashioned a Frankenstein monster that may shatter their livelihood.

? ? ? ? ? ? ? ? ? ? ? ?

1 Fill in the spaces
   a The General Strike happened in the year _____.
   b The miners belonged to a union called _____.
   c The miners' leader was _____.
   d The General Strike lasted _____ days.
   e The Government used _____ to do the trade unionists' jobs.
   f Trade unionists who tried to stop others going back to work were called _____.

2 The evidence here comes from people who were in favour of the strike, except for **K**. Explain how the evidence in **K** gives a different point of view. Whom do you agree with?

RAMSAY MACDONALD

A

January 1924 was a remarkable month in Britain. A new government took charge of British affairs. For the first time the country was going to be run by a new group – the Labour Party. Labour's leader, the new Prime Minister, came from Lossiemouth in north-east Scotland. His name was James Ramsay MacDonald, **A**.

MacDonald's rise to power was a great achievement. He spent his early life in a tiny two-roomed cottage. His father, a ploughman, never married his mother, Anne Ramsay. In 1866 she took her baby son and went to live with her own mother. The women found it a struggle to pay for the upkeep of a growing child. They had to find fees for his education, but were pleased to see young James proved to be a very able, hard working boy. MacDonald wrote about his schooldays

B *It was a steady hard grind to get at the heart of things. The teacher was impatient with what he called 'new fangled notions'. 'It is not what a man knows' he once said, 'but how he knows it that matters'.*

Night after night and morning after morning we took the long (4 mile) walk (to and from school) with Latin books or Greek open in our hands.

Because he was so successful at school MacDonald became a pupil teacher. From age 16 to 17 he earned £7 10s a year helping the teacher. He read books whenever he could.

C *In the neighbouring city there were booksellers' shops and thither I used to hasten to their windows. My beginnings in general reading were made standing there, reading. I used to walk 10 miles on Saturdays to do this. When I had a penny it was not to the booksellers I went, however. Their prices were not for me. There was a pawnbroker in the city and he sold me his 'rubbish' for next to nothing.*

MacDonald was very interested in how Britain was ruled. He joined a local society where meetings were held to discuss important events. Here he learned to speak in public. He later explained why he was attracted to groups who wanted to change Britain.

D *My childhood was lived at a time when the larger farmers were turning the people off the land. The whole of my part of Scotland was Radical. We looked down on people we called 'swells' and considered ourselves as good as, and a good deal better than, they were.*

MacDonald was too eager to change life in Britain to be able to settle down as a farm worker. He left home in 1885 and tried to find work first in Bristol, then London. Few of his jobs were well paid.

E *I used to buy myself food around the slums. I used to receive oatmeal, sent to me from home. I found hot water quite as good as tea. In the middle of the day I had a meal. I don't*

L

MacDonald's 'retreat' in Lossiemouth

think I ever spent more than twopence or threepence on it. My food bill worked out as sevenpence or eightpence a day for everything.

MacDonald joined groups that shared his interest in trying to improve life for ordinary people. In 1894 he joined a new group, the Independent Labour Party. He said

F *I ceased to trust in the Liberal Party when I was convinced that they were not prepared to go on and courageously face the bread and butter problems of the time, the problems of poverty, stunted lives and cruel conditions of work.*

MacDonald was one of the leaders who helped to create the Labour Party. In 1906 he was elected as Member of Parliament for Leicester. He was an impressive-looking man, a fine speaker and a very hard worker. He was ready to battle for causes that were not popular. His opposition to Britain's joining the Great War made his life very hard for a while. A friend, Molly Hamilton said

G *Those who got to know him thought he was an heroic figure, his courage was what struck us most. The first time I heard him was at a meeting in Bradford at which there was a tremendous rumpus from the back and it took a great deal of nerve to quell that rumpus and compel them to listen.*

MacDonald lived at a time when more people were getting the right to vote to choose MPs and when trade unions who supported his Labour Party were growing (see **H** and **J**).

The number of Labour MPs increased rapidly, **K**.

H **Who Could Vote to Choose MPs?**

Before 1918, about 60% of men over 21 years old.
In 1918, men over 21 and women over 30 years old.
In 1928, men and women over 21 years old.

J **The Growing Unions**

In 1900 there were 2 million trade unionists.
In 1914   ″   ″   4   ″   ″   ″
In 1920   ″   ″   8   ″   ″   ″

K **Number of Labour MPs, 1906 – 1929**

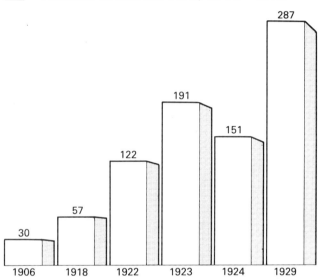

Year	MPs
1906	30
1918	57
1922	122
1923	191
1924	151
1929	287

Labour's success did not last long. By the end of 1924 the Party had lost power. But this was just the beginning of the Party's triumphs.

? ? ? ? ? ? ? ? ? ? ? ?

1 How do you think the information in **H** and **J** helps to explain the rise of the Labour Party?

2 Read **D** and **F**. Design a poster for one of MacDonald's election campaigns that will show what he, and the Labour Party, stood for.

3 From all you have read in this section, what do you think was the single most important reason for MacDonald's success? Give a reason for your answer.

OUT OF WORK

A shows a group of workers who have no jobs, standing about in the street. In the late 1920s and early 1930s sights like this were common. **B** gives some clues as to why this was. Scottish industry and Scottish farms suffered because foreign goods were cheaper and sometimes more up-to-date. A writer of the time noticed another reason:

C *Scotland has always depended more than England on the export market: the fall in world trade with its effect on shipbuilding, hurts coal, iron and steel.*

In 1932, 28% of all Scotland's workers had no job. Some parts suffered more than others. For example, in Stornoway 70% of workers had no job, in Wishaw 60% of workers were unemployed, and in Clydebank 54%. Shipbuilding workers were especially badly affected. One of their leaders explained to an English visitor how serious the situation was:

D *There are 120 000 unemployed in Glasgow, one in every three workers is out of work. The worst sufferers are the men engaged in shipbuilding and engineering. The River*

A

B **The decline of Scottish industries**

> In 1914 the Lanarkshire coalfield produced 17.5 million tons of coal.
>
> In 1937 the Lanarkshire coalfield produced 9 million tons of coal.
>
> 1904–14, the North British Locomotive Company made 400 engines a year.
>
> 1921–31, the North British Locomotive Company made 150 engines a year.
>
> 1932 the North British Locomotive Company made no engines.
>
> Between 1913 and 1935 the export of boilers fell by a half.

Clyde is crowded with idle ships for which there are no cargoes. Why build any more?

Men who lost their jobs found life a very hard struggle. A man who had been an hotel servant described the heartbreaking struggle to find a new job:

E *I spent much time and thought writing letters of application which I posted at two a week. My feet became weary, my boots worn and leaky: my meals which were few and far between consisted mostly of tea, bread and margarine. I used to listen eagerly every morning for the postman's knock. One bleak miserable day I decided to pawn my best suit. With the money I enjoyed a few satisfactory meals. Other articles were pawned including my watch until there came the day when I had nothing left to pawn. A terrible feeling of despair gripped me.*

Many people took their possessions to pawnbrokers who allowed them money but kept the goods if the customer couldn't find the cash to reclaim what they had left in the pawnshop.

The government paid a small sum called 'the dole' to the unemployed. Its inspectors checked that people really were very poor. A Dundee woman, Sarah Craig, hated these visits, as did most unemployed people:

F *Mr Allan, he came and he looked round. 'Can you no' sell this, can you no' sell that'.*

G

They would even lift the lid off where you kept your coal.

Housewives had to be very careful if they were to manage on the dole. In some places men had to carry out jobs before they could receive it **G**. In **H** you can see how one family spent their money.

The large number of unemployed dropped slowly in the later 1930s as Britain re-armed for war. But the problems only vanished when the Second World War began.

H	How a Greenock family of ten people spent their dole of £1.19.3 a week		
Rent	12/-	Sugar	10d
Gas	3/-	Bread	7/-
Societies (to save		Meat	2/10
for clothes and		Vegetables	11d
doctors' bills)	1/4	Rice	4d
Coal	2/3	Dripping	3d
Milk	2/4	Tea-bread	6d
Soap	8d	Fish	10d
Potatoes	2/-	Biscuits	4d
Margarine	1/-	Salt and pepper	1d
Tea	9d		

?????????????

1 From **B,C** and **D** write out a list of the jobs most badly affected by unemployment.

2 Look at **H**.
a What was the costliest item in the budget?
b What do you think they probably ate a great deal of to keep away hunger?
c What is missing from the list but would usually be on your family's weekly shopping list?

3 'A Pawnkeeper's Day' 1932
Under this heading imagine you are the keeper of a pawnshop and describe one day's business as if you are writing a diary. Mention different people who have come to your shop. They explain why they need help; they bring different things to pawn. At least one customer comes to pay you back and recover his possession. He tells you how he has made money. Decorate your story with a pawn-keeper's sign.

LIVING IN A GLASGOW TENEMENT

In 1921 a little over a million people lived in Glasgow. 65.5% of them lived in homes consisting of just one or two rooms.

Molly Weir lived in Glasgow with her two brothers, her mother and her Grannie in the 1920s and 30s. Her home was part of a larger building called a *tenement*, **A**. This is how she described it:

B   *We called our room and kitchen a 'house', for we'd never heard of the word 'flat' when I was a wee girl. It was in a red sandstone tenement . . . The tenements were all lit by gas . . . An outside toilet had to be shared with two other families. There were several large families living in a single room. One family had 14 children and they all lived in one room with a box-like compartment leading out of it.*

The tenements were crowded with families. Each family was only able to afford the rent if at least one person worked very hard to earn a wage. In Molly's case it was her mother:

C   *My mother painted railway wagons. Hard, heavy work for a slight creature like her but she was glad to get it. At lunch-time the horns were the signal for our street to be filled with the crunch of hundreds upon hundreds of tramping feet as the railway workers hurried home for their dinner. No canteen meals for them. Nobody used buses or trams. Everybody walked.*

The workers came home to meals cooked on large black kitchen ranges, like **D**. Molly explained

E   *It was the centre of warmth and comfort. Every bit was used for cooking. The kettle was always on the side and only needed moving over the flames to bring it to boiling for tea or pease brose. Beef tea sat simmering at the back of the hob. The big soup pot stood at the other side. The stew pot wasn't far away and there was still room for the pot that held potatoes.*

There were many small shops near the tenements, but one was more important than the rest.

F   *The Co-operative Store was the hub of our shopping activities. Along one side ran the long mahogany counter with female clerks perched on high stools whose job it was to write down our orders. Along the opposite side ran the long wooden counter attended by the serving grocers, usually male. In the back shop potatoes were housed in a huge bunker which had a sliding door in the front for the 'tattie boy' to push in his shovel and rattle down the necessary amount. Eggs were very precious. Everything that was bought in the Co-op was marked in the book and no money changed hands until pay day. Two doors down was the drapery department which also sold shoes. Shoes were worn only on Sundays. There was a Co-op about*

A

every 500 yards in our district. In those busy shops in pre-refrigerator days shopping had to be done every day.

The tenement families had to be very careful with the small amount of money they had to spend.

G *We learned never to waste a thing. When I was old enough to empty the sugar bags Grannie showed me how to fold back the corners so that it was smooth and not a grain of sugar lost . . . I used to trot into town with the daughter of a neighbour for there was a shop which sold ham bones for twopence ha'penny for two pairs which gave them two good pots of lentil soup and a good picking at the bones with their boiled potatoes. It was a mile and a half each way but we thought nothing of it . . . Apart from my boots practically everything was hand made and mostly of things first worn by my mother or somebody else.*

The tenements did not have bathrooms or space in the kitchen where clothes could be washed. Molly described where washing was done

H *The wash house was in the back court and each one served the 12 families in each tenement close. Our tenement women all had raw fingers from using the slimy black soap and soda. I loved when things were judged to be ready. The heavy boiler lid was lifted off. Clouds of steam rushed everywhere. The washer, a long pole in both hands fished out a load, expertly twirling the steaming clothes, and ran to the tub of clean water. Back and forth she went, her figure ghost-like in the rushing steam. It was a great source of pride to have someone say 'Aye, she hangs out a lovely washing'.*

Children often played in the street as well as the back court **J**. Since their families could not afford expensive toys they had to make up games that used the things they found in the area. But there were occasional treats to eat.

K *Sometimes Grannie would spread two pieces of thin white bread with fresh margarine . . . A 'piece' on chips was at once filling and exciting. Another treat was a piece on condensed milk. A piece on black treacle was a rare delight . . . We never aspired to a sandwich in the true sense. We never dreamt of meat or cheese or eggs.*

Life in the tenements was hard, but it was never lonely. People helped one another, there were many neighbours to chat to and Molly Weir had plenty of other children to play with.

? ? ? ? ? ? ? ? ? ? ? ?

1 This section includes many clues that show that people living in the tenements did not have much money. Find and write out six of these clues.

2 Why did people go shopping every day, **F**?

3 Look at **F**. Family orders for a week's food were written down in Co-op order books. Set out a whole page as if it were part of one of these books. Write in the name of the family. From what you have read in this chapter fill in the page as if it were the Weirs' weekly order.

POPULAR PASTIMES

In the 1920s radios first appeared. Richard Penner remembered how excited he was when he first listened to one:

A *Late in 1924 every boy we knew seemed to be making a crystal wireless receiver. I had never heard wireless before and it was a wonderful moment when Bob handed me the earphones and said proudly 'Listen – music.' I was so thrilled I jumped up, moved the set and of course lost the station.*

By this time people could also enjoy going to the cinema **B**. A great number were built in the 1920s and '30s. By 1929 in Glasgow alone there were 127 cinemas. Crowds queued to see popular stars of the time like Charlie Chaplin. Most children went to special cinema programmes every Saturday.

C *I used to get in almost every Saturday for two one-pound jam jars. (A halfpenny was the return you got from the grocer for a clean jam jar.) It was a penny to get in.*

The villain had to make an entrance at least once every five minutes.

'Look, the man's got a knife! Mind yer back Jimmy!'

The hero was saved by the audience – and he never paid any attention! We all enjoyed our-selves enormously. We were probably quite outrageous in the noise we made, but it was nothing but kids. It was plain wooden forms. There was no such thing as ice-cream. A lot of hard caramels were chewed and stuck down the lassies' jerseys.

D *For a penny we not only saw the show but sometimes received either a free comic or small bag of sweets as well. The entire programme must have lasted under the hour and comprised a 'funny' and an episode of such serials as 'The Hooded Terror' or 'Tarzan'. The merits of various cinemas were widely discussed. Our local was dismissed as a 'Flea-pit'. I gathered that there were cinemas actually fitted with individual seats instead of benches.*

The 1920s and '30s were also a golden age for Scottish soccer. Huge crowds went every Saturday to see their favourite teams. The crowd in **E** are going to watch Aberdeen. The men who played for the most important clubs were not well paid by today's standards. But at the time they believed themselves very lucky. Jerry Dawson (a goalkeeper) explains why this was so:

F *I signed for Rangers in the season 1929–30. My parents were not at all keen on*

Children queuing outside a Glasgow cinema in the 1930s

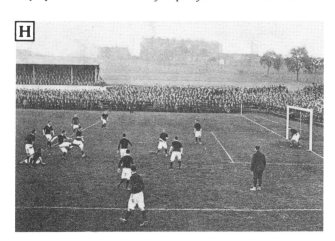

my playing professional football. We were subject to very strict physical and social disciplines. Don't swim in fresh water, don't play badminton, be very smart on the field. To lose one's place in the side was almost certainly to return to the Labour Exchange. We played in the palmy days of football. In the circumstances of the time we were millionaires. We made about £15 a week.

Scottish footballers played in much heavier equipment than today's players. It included:

G Iron-toed boots, laces that would have tied a liner securely to a dock, long-john pants, shinguards that turned legs into supports for a snooker table and jerseys as old fashioned as granny's bathing costume.

Picture **H** gives a glimpse of the footballers' clothing. This match was between Dundee and Hearts.

1 Look at the photographs on these pages. What clues in them tell you that they are not modern pictures?

2 Design a cinema poster for one of the films mentioned in **D**. Include the price on the poster.

3 From **F** what sort of background do you think most Scottish footballers came from?

A SERVANT'S LIFE

In your home there are probably several machines to help do the housework of cooking, cleaning and washing. Imagine the time it would take to do all these jobs if you did not have gas or electricity. Many of these inventions have only become common since the 1930s. The cooker in advertisement **A** was very modern at the time. Before then people who could afford it paid servants to do their housework. Until the Great War there were more women working as domestic servants than in any other job. The written evidence in this section all comes from people who worked at 'the Big House' on one Highland estate in the 1920s and '30s.

B *The scullery maid and kitchen maid had to rise at 4.45 every morning and come down to clean the two huge grates in the kitchen; flue them, blacklead them, polish until all the bits shone. The scullery maid had then to go and wash the long passage from the servants' dining hall to the back door. The kitchen maid was getting things organized for the cook, putting out oatmeal for porridge, getting the pot on the fire . . . Staff breakfast was porridge and milk and rolls. Most of the gentry ate porridge and probably kidney and sausage, bacon and egg, maybe fish.*

Then it was time for the scullery maid to wash and dry. The lady would give orders for lunch. Dinner was at 8.15 and often the gentry were never out of the dining room until after 10.30. And there was still washing up to be done. The scullery maid had 10 shillings a week plus meals, board and uniform; the kitchen maid was getting 15 shillings and the cook had £1.10.0d.

The average lunch would be a 4 or 5 course affair. It was similar at dinner with a fish course between the soup and the meat. The gents were then left to their glass of port and the ladies went through for coffee. After half an hour they all got together again, they usually played cards.

Jessie Gordon, scullery maid

C *As a kitchen maid I had to wear a pale green linen frock with a green apron while the cook was dressed in a black frock and white apron. The cook would inspect me as if I was a soldier on parade. We all had 2 weeks off a year.*

Agnes Black, kitchen maid

D is a photograph of a cook and a parlour-maid in the 1930s, wearing the sort of uniforms described in **C**.

E *One of my main grumbles in my late teens and early 20s was the ridiculously early hour I was expected to be back at the Big House if I had an evening off. We each had a day off a week and unless you had asked special permission we had to be back by 9pm.*

Grace Macarthur, housemaid

F *I had to put on my uniform when acting as chauffeur. I drove all sorts, the good and the bad. The ill mannered ones gave the impression that you were no better than dirt under their feet. I found as a chauffeur it was easier to get along with the laird than with his wife. She was very much the upper-class lady. You were just the servant in her eyes.* John Jameson, chauffeur

G is an advertisement for the kind of car John Jameson might have driven.

H *When I started work as a laundry maid I felt really proud. All estates had their own laundry. Inside there were a number of rooms. The main one was where all the washing was done in wooden tubs. Next to this was the drying room where the laundry was hung up. The other main room was the ironing room where we all worked with heavy irons heated from a big stove in the centre of the floor. With the stove on full blast to heat the water in the boilers and all the tubs full, with the steam gushing out like smoke, it was like being in one of those greenhouses.* Janet Gray, laundry maid

J *There were times when you felt a very separate person; not quite on a level with your employer and at some distance from the rest of the staff . . . I had my own separate quarters . . . The governess did not eat with the rest of the staff. She always dined in the nursery with the children. The normal pattern was that the children would be in the care of a nanny from birth until the age of 5. At this stage I would take over. I taught them reading, writing, mathematics, history, geography, piano playing, violin playing, harp playing, sewing and knitting. A room in the nursery wing was set aside as a schoolroom and fitted with desks and a blackboard. It was always a sad day for me when they reached the age of 12 or 13 and boarding schools had to be found for them.*

Dorothy Saunders, governess

K *There was never any fear of losing your house or your job providing you did your work. We had our own dairy with milk a penny a pint.*

G

CITROËN
"BIG 12" 4 CYLINDER   "TWENTY" 6 CYLINDER
—IMPROVED CHASSIS —FINER PERFORMANCE —IMPROVED COACHWORK
—WIDER AND BETTER BODIES   (FULL 5 OR 7 SEATER)

1932 Citroen "Big 12" 4-Cylinder 5-Seater Saloon de Luxe (Sliding Roof) with Bendix 4-Wheel Brakes, etc.

"BIG 12"—Rear Petrol Tank; Improved and More Powerful Engine; Improved Performance; Increased Acceleration; Improved Starter; New Carburetter for easy starting; Breathing Device to prevent crankcase dilution; Bendix Duo-Servo 4-wheel Brakes; Wider Track (4 ft. 8 in.); More Luxurious Interiors; Lower and Wider Bodies; Specially Wide Doors; New Bumpers and Grid; Dipping Headlamp Reflectors; Glove Box; Window Ventilating Louvres; and Glass Sun Visor on De-Luxe Models; Wire or Disc Wheels, with large Hubs; Spare Wheel at side.

"TWENTY"—Rear Petrol Tank; More Powerful Engine improved as on "Big 12"; De-Luxe Equipment as above; Bonnet of new design; Chromium-plated Radiator Shutters with Thermostatic control; Larger Tyres; New Unique Flexible Bumpers; Scuttle-Dash Side Lamps.

"BIG TWELVE" Prices from £195   "TWENTY" Prices from £295

S. M. T. LOTHIAN ROAD SHOWROOMS
71 LOTHIAN ROAD, EDINBURGH
'Phone 25136

Potatoes — we could have as many as we liked for nothing. Everybody kept hens, the houses all had good gardens. Although the wages were small it really was a happy contented life. I think that television has not been the best of influences in the country districts. It makes people want to get away to the brighter lights . . . People have become lazy now. They'll never think about cycling anywhere. Local shops have closed.

Donald Watson, estate worker

THE BLITZ

Between 1939 and 1945 Britain and Germany were once more at war. Men left home to join the forces. But the people who stayed at home were in danger too. German aircraft flew over Scottish cities dropping bombs. One of the worst of these 'blitz' attacks happened on 13 and 14 March, 1941. Over 200 German bombers attacked the homes and factories of Clydebank.

The people of Clydebank lived in one or two roomed homes in tall tenement buildings. One of them remembers how the raid began:

A *The siren went about 9 o'clock in the evening and at home my mother was in, my 2 sisters and myself and we thought it was just another raid. The sirens had gone before and nothing had ever happened. But before many minutes had passed things began to fall down from the wall, glass splintering and my mother decided that we'd better really go downstairs into the close.*

Some people were not at home. When the raid started they ran home to try and find shelter:

B *I ran home all the way. Through the school which was blazing, the wood yard blazing, collected my little girl and went into my own house. We decided to gather up cushions and cover ourselves.*

There were small air raid shelters scattered about the town. Some people crowded into these. They tried to keep their minds off the terrible sounds of the raid:

C *We used to sit in the shelters and play guessing games and sing, and then 'I spy' — I used to laugh — 'I spy' in the dark! We'd light candles and once we got the 'I spy', the candle would be put out again. And then sing-songs, it was all the old fashioned songs.*

When the raid was over people came out of their homes and their shelters. Their town lay in ruins, **D**. Rescue workers began to clear up, **E**. Many people now had no home to go to. They tried to find their possessions, **F**.

Russell Hunter lived in a Clydebank tenement with his mother. After the blitz they came out of the shelter and returned home.

G *To be in that shelter was something. It was like being in a darkened telephone box.(When) we went upstairs in the morning there were no windows, no internal walls, the only thing – the budgie was still alive. It was under the table. It was black. It used to chatter away. But it never regained its colour and it was dumb. No wonder! The poor wee thing had lived through a blitz.*

My mother had a souvenir. It was a tiny crystal cream jug. And through it, from one side to the other, driven through it, was an arrow head of window glass. And there was no crack in the jug.

I was unfortunate enough to have to drag a few bodies out.

There seemed to be little of Clydebank left **H**. Rescue workers fought to tackle the destruction:

J *We only had about 10 rescue teams, perhaps 10 fire engines, half a dozen ambulances, perhaps 10 first aid parties. We just couldn't cope. The telephones went, we were dependent on runners. And these were just young lads. So communication was hopeless. There were fires*

F

H **Destruction caused by the Blitz on Clydebank**

4300 houses completely destroyed
7700 houses damaged
8 houses undamaged
534 people killed
790 people seriously injured

all over the place. Sometimes an explosion had broken a gas main and set the gas alight. My impression was the whole town was on fire and very little was being done about it.

The people who survived the blitz never forgot it. Bridget McHard is just one of many survivors with a very sad tale to tell:

K *I had three sisters, three brothers – there was five of them killed in the Blitz and my father was killed in the Blitz as well. It was really only my mother and I that survived out of the building.*

? ? ? ? ? ? ? ? ? ? ?

1 The evidence in this section describes several ways in which the blitz affected Clydebank. What damage do you think the German bombers meant to cause? Complete the following orders, as if you were a German leader planning the raid.
'Raid on Clydebank, Scotland. March 13th/ 14th, 1941. Air crew will search for the following targets _____. Bombing will begin at _____ hours.'

2 Imagine you are a rescue worker like the man in **E**. You are filling in a report to note down the work you have done:
'March 15th, 1941
Report of _____ of the Air Raid Police. During the past two days I have _____'

Continue the report. Mention the people you have helped, and how you have helped them. Mention your work in guiding rescue services to where they are needed. Note down how much damage you think has been done. Suggest what will need to be done to restore life to normal.

WARTIME LIFE, 1939–45

Scotland's local newspapers contain clues about everyday life in wartime. The evidence in this section comes from Aberdeen's *Press and Journal*. The war brought food shortages. The government tackled this problem by deciding how much food and clothing everyone was allowed. Ration books consisted of pages of 'coupons' to be handed over whenever anything was bought, **A**. Britain's people had to grow more food. Even Scotland's precious golf courses suffered, **B**. Women had to take over farm work once done by men, **C**.

Some people who lived in areas the Germans were likely to bomb went to safer country areas. Most of these *evacuees* were children. They did not all like the countryside, **D**. **E** is part of an advertisement. Why would people try to stop light showing through their windows at night?

Some foods weren't rationed, **F** and **G**. The Germans sank so many ships bringing goods to Britain that people had to collect waste and scrap, **H** and **J**. Advertisers tried to persuade people that their goods were especially helpful to the war effort **K**. By the time the war ended people were very ready to celebrate **L**. They had suffered a long period of danger and shortages.

A January 1940

REASONS FOR RATIONING

War has meant the re-planning of our food supplies. Half our meat and most of our bacon, butter and sugar come from overseas. Here are 4 reasons for rationing.
1 Rationing prevents waste of food.
2 Rationing increases our war effort. To cut our food purchases abroad frees ships to bring other imports.
3 Rationing divides supplies equally.
4 Rationing prevents uncertainty. Your ration book assures you of your fair share!

B March 1941

GOLF COURSES TO BE PLOUGHED

Golf courses are to be ploughed to make their contribution to the kitchen front campaign. It is hoped to leave the greater part of courses still for play. At Hazlehead, Aberdeen, about 20 acres of the new course will be ploughed.

C August 1941

LAND GIRLS

'This year's harvest is important to us' said Sir Patrick Laird in an appeal for recruits to the Women's Land Army. In the last month the number of land girls in Scotland had risen to 1300.

D May 1940

WHY SOME EVACUEES WANT HOME

When war broke out Peterculter (Aberdeenshire) received 813 evacuees; now there are only 40. One reason was lack of entertainment. 3 ladies and their children were offered homes in the village of Garlogie. When they got there they refused to leave the car which had taken them from the station. There was no cinema in the village. 'We dinna like bizzin' bees and coos' they said. They returned to Glasgow.'

E

BUY NOW WHILE IT LASTS

BLACK FELT for blackout purposes, suitable for windows, glass doors etc. – 5 pence a yard. BLACK PAPER. Can be attached to blinds – 3 pence a yard. P. Scrogie, Peterhead.

F January 1940

Tatties, Herrin' and Oatcakes Cheap

Scotland's traditional food such as tatties, herrin', porridge and oatcakes can play a part in winning the war. 'There is a big surplus of potatoes in Scotland' said the Food Controller for the North East. Both are rich in food value and cheap to buy.

G

December 1940

Use Carrots

We now know that carrots are even better than they look. They protect us against illnesses, give us energy and act as a tonic. Carrots will hclp to eke out your Christmas fare. They contain a certain amount of sugar so should serve as a sugar ration saver as well as a source of extra nourishment in cakes and puddings.

'Carrots not your idea of a breakfast dish?' asks Dr Carrot. 'Just try my carrot marmalade!'.

H

UP HOUSEWIVES AND AT 'EM

Housewives of Britain. You have a great part to play. Your country needs your waste paper, bones and metal. They help to make vital war supplies. You are striking a blow for your homes and your children when you save every bit of paper, bone and metal and put it out carefully. Go into action today. Paper makes rifle shell cases, food containers. Bones make glue for aeroplanes and fertilizers for crops. Metal makes aeroplanes, tanks, guns, ships.

J

October 1940

Waste in school books. A reader's letter.

Dear Sir,

Allow me to draw the attention of teachers to the waste that is openly found in children's home-work books. The other night I was looking over my son's arithmetic book and found that the teacher makes pupils spread one tiny sum over a whole page, three quarters of the page being wasted. To draw the teacher's attention to this waste I wrote in big letters "WASTE. WAR ON!" What's wrong with the good old-fashioned slate to do sums on?

Angry Parent.

L

April 1945

Aberdeen will celebrate Victory with 2 Days of Gaiety

Aberdeen will celebrate victory with bonfires, fire-works, decorations, band music, open-air dancing and thanksgiving services.

Church bells ringing, air raid sirens sounding a five minute 'all-clear' and the hoot of sirens from ships in the habour will herald the great news.

At night bonfires will blaze. If possible there will be a firework display.

It is hoped that full street lighting will be resumed. The Town Hall will set the example of flag flying and tram cars will also fly bunting.

School children will be given a holiday.

K You should just taste this Custard Pudding

MAKE IT WITHOUT EGGS!

Once you've tried this lovely Creamola, you'll wonder why you ever used eggs to make an egg custard pudding. So will everybody. For if ever a pudding made us all kiddies again it's this real custard treat.

And creamy, delicious Creamola makes a " set " custard pudding — served hot or cold. Of course you can, if you wish, make it into a pouring custard.

MEAT RATIONING. A little less meat and a little more Creamola will hurt nobody. In fact, Mother, Creamola is so nourishing that it will help you get through on your food money with every-body satisfied and happy.

THERE ARE 3 KINDS OF CREAMOLA

Custard Pudding

Rice Custard Pudding

EACH 3d. PACKET MAKES 3 CUSTARD PUDDINGS — EACH PUDDING IS ENOUGH FOR 4 GOOD HELPINGS!

Sago Custard Pudding

Creamola Food Products Ltd., Glasgow, S.1

CREAMOLA
CUSTARD PUDDINGS

????????????

1 Search the evidence to find the answers to the following:

a How can you tell that oranges were in short supply?

b What clue tells you that wartime streets were very dark?

c What sound warned people that there was going to be an air raid?

d What sort of foods were not rationed?

2 The war in your area. Can any people in your area remember the war? Plan questions to put to people who can remember rationing, shortages, bombing and evacuees.

3 Look at **F**. Design a simple bold poster that will catch people's attention to tell them to save waste and scrap. *OR* Look at **C**. Design a poster to persuade women to join the Women's Land Army.

4 The evidence in this section comes from newspapers. It is very helpful. But news-papers were not allowed to print everything they wanted. Can you think of any evidence about the war that you would *not* find in newspapers?

SCOTTISH LIFE: MAP

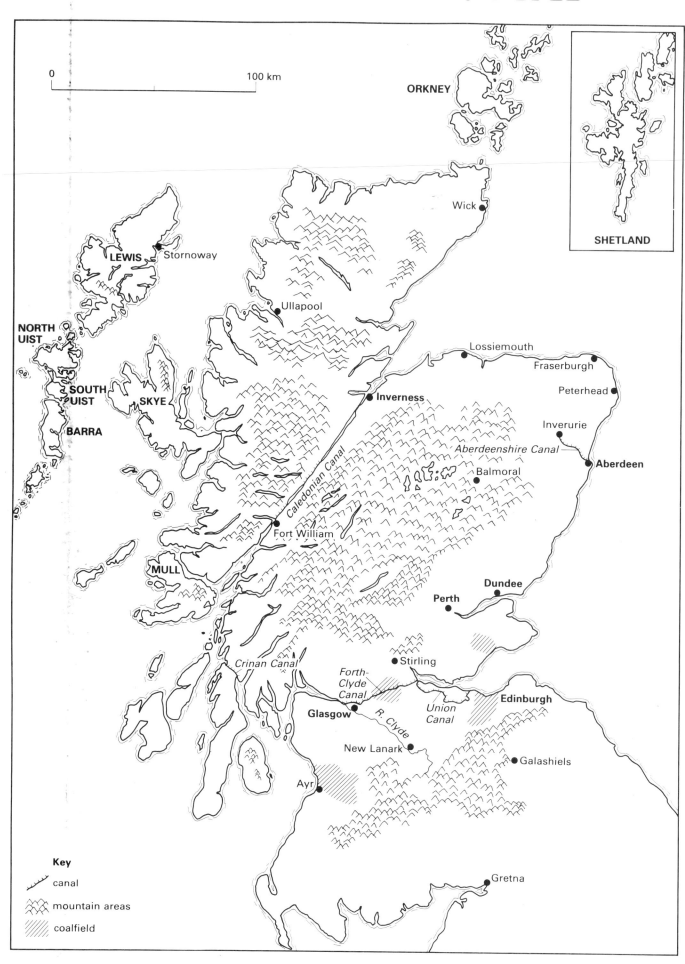

0   100 km

ORKNEY

Wick

SHETLAND

LEWIS Stornoway

Ullapool

NORTH UIST

Lossiemouth

Fraserburgh

SOUTH UIST

SKYE **Inverness**

Peterhead

BARRA

Inverurie

Aberdeenshire Canal **Aberdeen**

Balmoral

Caledonian Canal

Fort William

MULL

Dundee

Perth

Stirling

Crinan Canal

Forth-Clyde Canal **Edinburgh**

Glasgow *R. Clyde* *Union Canal*

New Lanark

Galashiels

Ayr

Gretna

Key

canal

mountain areas

coalfield

64